Realism and Idealism in Wilson's Peace Program

EDWIN C. ROZWENC, Ph.D.

*Chairman, Department of American Studies
Amherst College*

THOMAS LYONS

*Department of History
Phillips Academy, Andover, Massachusetts*

D. C. HEATH AND COMPANY

BOSTON · ENGLEWOOD · CHICAGO · SAN FRANCISCO
ATLANTA · DALLAS · LONDON · TORONTO

32733

973·913

COPYRIGHT © 1965 BY D. C. HEATH AND COMPANY

No part of the material covered by this copyright may be reproduced in any form without written permission of the publisher. (6 K 4)

PRINTED IN THE UNITED STATES OF AMERICA
22480

TABLE OF CONTENTS

THE words "realist" and "idealist" are two of the more commonplace labels that invariably creep into our conversations about politics. And, although most people never make any serious effort to define these words, they cannot be dismissed as additional examples of the confused and hazy vocabulary of the mythical man-in-the-street. Indeed, most political scientists would agree that the distinction between "realism" and "idealism" is an extremely useful one for political thought, even though it is not easy to define clearly what is meant by these terms.

In political usage, "realism" is most commonly ascribed to those political leaders or political theorists who are primarily concerned with sober and hard-nosed facts—the "what is" of history and politics. On the other hand, "idealism" is used to describe those political leaders or thinkers who are mainly concerned with their hopes for a better life or a better world—the "what ought to be" of history and politics.

Two examples will remind us how deeply embedded these two concepts are in our heritage of political thought. Plato, the great Greek philosopher, stated the position of the idealist in the *Republic* when he wrote: "We are inquiring into the

Part 1

The Concepts of Realism and Idealism

nature of absolute justice and into the character of the perfectly just . . . that we might have an ideal. . . . And is our theory a worse theory because we are unable to prove the possibility of a city being ordered in the manner described?" Machiavelli, a great writer and political thinker of the Renaissance period in European history, stated the position of the realist in *The Prince* when he wrote: ". . . there is such a difference between the way men live and the way they ought to live, that anybody who abandons what is for what ought to be will learn something that will ruin rather than preserve him, because anyone who determines to act in all circumstances the part of a good man must come to ruin among many who are not good. Hence, if a prince wishes to maintain himself, he must learn to be not good, and to use that ability or not as is required."

Although we can find such clear distinctions in classic writings of political theory, we must not allow ourselves to fall into the pedantic error of assuming that we will find many political leaders in the real world of politics who can be contrasted so neatly in their behavior. Many political leaders whom we might readily call "realists" often take the moral and spiritual values of their society into serious consideration when they make their decisions. Similarly, most political leaders whom we might label as "idealists" have to reckon with the established institutions of their societies—whether they include privileged churches, feudal oligarchies, industrial monopolies, entrenched bureaucracies, party machines, or mass media of communication.

Consequently, the difference between realism and idealism often tends to become blurred or shaded, especially when we observe the behavior of man in concrete historical situations. Yet the distinction can be useful and valid, particularly if we add a few more terms to our conceptual framework. When we take a closer look at the realist in politics, we discover that he is likely to be a person whose ideas and actions are firmly rooted in his recognition that a struggle for power and positions of power exists in every human society. The idealist, on the other hand, either disregards such power problems, or, if he does recognize them, he tries to look beyond them toward new goals and solutions that will transcend the existing struggles for power and positions of power. Thus, if we want to make effective use of the distinction between realists and idealists as an analytic tool, we must try to determine the degree to which a political leader shapes his goals with considerations of self-interest—of egoistic strivings for prestige, wealth, power and survival—rather than with expectations that look beyond mere self-preservation and self-interest.

The history of the United States offers rich possibilities for an examination of the interaction between realistic and idealistic motives in politics. Such different tendencies were present in the party battles between Hamiltonian Federalists and Jeffersonian Republicans and have continued in almost every generation since the founding of the American Republic.

Moreover, the same kind of conflict between realistic and idealistic purposes has shaped the development of foreign policy throughout our history. Indeed, it was Alexander Hamilton who first reminded his countrymen that the new American republic could not escape the harsh necessities of a foreign policy based on egoistic considerations of the national interest. "The rule of morality," he wrote, ". . . is not precisely the same between nations as between individuals. . . . Whence it follows that an individual may, on numerous occasions, meritoriously indulge the emotions of generosity and benevolence . . . even at the expense of his own interest. But a government can rarely, if at all, be justifiable in pursuing a similar course." On the other hand, Jefferson hoped that America could develop a new kind of foreign policy. He believed that America was destined "by nature" and "a wide ocean" to be free of "the exterminating wars of Europe;" and he hoped that we might create "a different code of natural law to govern relations with other nations from that which the conditions of Europe have given rise to there."

In our own century, this classic conflict between realistic and idealistic tendencies in American foreign policy has been shaped most significantly by our involvement in the efforts of peacemaking after two world wars that were more bloody and more destructive than any in previous human history. And Woodrow Wilson, more than any other man, caused his generation, as well as that which followed, to confront the dilemmas posed by the conflicting demands of realism and idealism.

Although the United States was drawn into the first World War largely because our national interest was menaced by Germany's unrestricted submarine warfare, President Wilson sought to define our objectives with higher principles than those of material interest. In his major public addresses, especially those in which he elaborated his famous Fourteen Points, he called for a peace after the war was won that would not be based on military alliances and a new balance of power, but rather on a new code of international morality that would be supported by an international organization to be called the League of Nations.

President Wilson's conceptions of peacemaking brought him into conflict with other political leaders at home and abroad. In the Peace Conference at Versailles, Wilson confronted such men as David Lloyd George, the prime minister of England, and Georges Clemenceau, the leader of the French government, who were thoroughly imbued with the traditions of European diplomacy. At home he faced the opposition of such political leaders as Theodore Roosevelt and Henry Cabot Lodge who insisted that American foreign policy should be built upon considerations of power and self-interest.

Indeed, there are no other events in the history of American foreign policy that can match, in their dramatic intensity, the battles that Wilson fought: first with the leaders of the Allied Powers in Paris over the provisions of the Treaty of Versailles and the Covenant of the League of Nations, and then with the leaders of the opposition in the United States Senate over the ratification of the treaty and the covenant. And despite the defeat of the treaty and the covenant in the United States Senate, subsequent events—a second world war, the creation of a United Nations organization, and the emergence of a large number of new nations by a process of self-determination—suggest that Wilsonian ideals may have been more compatible with the realities of the twentieth century world than Wilson's generation was willing to recognize.

Thus, the main problem that we shall be exploring in this volume is suggested by the following questions: *Did Wilson fail at Paris? Were his ideas of peacemaking too rational and moralistic? Did he demand a greater sacrifice of national interests than the people of America and Europe could give, or did he point the way toward the kind of international order that was indispensable in the changing conditions of the twentieth century?*

To help us answer these questions, the readings in this volume include selections from Woodrow Wilson's public papers in which he states his proposals for a just and lasting peace. In addition, there are several statements made by Wilson's critics and opponents in the United States and Europe. Finally, there are several selections written by historians and political scientists that will enable us to see how some leading scholars have attempted to appraise Wilson's foreign policy.

As we confront the questions raised in connection with the readings in this volume, we can see that many of them are still with us today. Various surveys of public opinion show that the American people still have abiding aspirations for world peace, for the elimination of tyranny and the promotion of democracy, and for the abolition of poverty, disease, and illiteracy among all peoples. Much of the energy and imagination of American leadership is still devoted to the task of translating these aspirations into practical measures and policies. In short, we are still testing the adequacy of many Wilsonian principles in the development of our foreign policy.

OUR first step toward discovering the relationship between idealism and realism in Woodrow Wilson's diplomacy will be to examine four of his speeches on the subject of peacemaking. In this connection, we must remember that Wilson's thoughts about a just and lasting peace did not suddenly spring, full-blown as it were, from his mind; they were hammered out over a period of three or four years in response to the circumstances of the European war before and after America's entry. Consequently, the four speeches that we shall read represent four important stages in the development of Wilson's ideas. The first selection represents Wilson's early proposals during the period of American neutrality. The second gives us Wilson's thoughts at the intensely dramatic moment when he called upon Congress and the American people to go to war against Germany. The third selection provides us with his most ambitious effort to spell out specific points for a peace settlement. And the final selection is a defense of the Treaty and the League Covenant after he had faced the severe battering of controversy and conflict at the Paris Peace Conference. These four documents will supply us with the essential principles of Wilson's peacemaking diplomacy.

Part 2

Wilsonian Principles of Peacemaking

1. WOODROW WILSON: "PEACE WITHOUT VICTORY"

For more than a year before the United States declared war against Germany, Woodrow Wilson tried to use the moral force of the United States to lead the warring nations of Europe toward negotiations that might bring a just and lasting peace. After the sinking of the Lusitania *by a German submarine, President Wilson realized that the best way to keep America out of the European war was to help bring it to an end. When the war reached a stalemate in the autumn of 1916, he was convinced that the opportunity had come for a neutral America to serve as a mediator. On December 18, 1916, he sent identical notes to the Central Powers and the Allied Powers, asking them to state the terms on which they would be willing to stop fighting. While waiting for their replies, President Wilson went before the Senate to describe the kind of settlement that he hoped could be achieved. The selection below is taken from his address to the Senate, delivered on January 22, 1917. Read it carefully and consider the following questions:*

1. Why does Wilson think that the United States, a neutral nation, should try to play a part in organizing a peace settlement?
2. Why is Wilson opposed to a peace built on the concept of "a balance of power"?
3. What does he mean when he suggests the idea of a "community of power"? By what means can a "peace without victory" be guaranteed?

. . . I have sought this opportunity to address you because I thought that I owed it to you, as the counsel associated with me in the final determination of our international obligations, to disclose to you without reserve the thought and purpose that have been taking form in my mind in regard to the duty of our Government in the days to come when it will be necessary to lay afresh and upon a new plan the foundations of peace among the nations.

From Ray Stannard Baker and William E. Dodd, eds., *The Public Papers of Woodrow Wilson*, Vol. 4, pp. 407–410. Cprt. Edith B. Wilson, 1926.

It is inconceivable that the people of the United States should play no part in that great enterprise. To take part in such a service will be the opportunity for which they have sought to prepare themselves by the very principles and purposes of their polity and the approved practices of their Government ever since the days when they set up a new nation in the high and honorable hope that it might in all that it was and did show mankind the way to liberty. They cannot in honor withhold the service to which they are now about to be challenged. They do not wish to withhold it. But they owe it to themselves and to the other nations of the world to state the conditions under which they will feel free to render it.

That service is nothing less than this, to add their authority and their power to the authority and force of other nations to guarantee peace and justice throughout the world. Such a settlement cannot now be long postponed. It is right that before it comes this Government should frankly formulate the conditions upon which it would feel justified in asking our people to approve its formal and solemn adherence to a League for Peace. I am here to attempt to state those conditions.

The present war must first be ended; but we owe it to candor and to a just regard for the opinion of mankind to say that, so far as our participation in guarantees of future peace is concerned, it makes a great deal of difference in what way and upon what terms it is ended. The treaties and agreements which bring it to an end must embody terms which will create a peace that is worth guaranteeing and preserving, a peace that will win the approval of mankind, not merely a peace that will serve the several interests and immediate aims of the nations engaged. We shall have no voice in determining what those terms shall be, but we shall, I feel sure, have a voice in determining whether they shall be made lasting or not by the guarantes of a universal covenant, and our judgment upon what is fundamental and essential as a condition precedent to permanency should be spoken now, not afterwards when it may be too late.

No covenant of co-operative peace that does not include the peoples of the New World can suffice to keep the future safe against war; and yet there is only one sort of peace that the peoples of America could join in guaranteeing. The elements of that peace must be elements that engage the confidence and satisfy the principles of the American governments, elements consistent with their political faith and with the practical convictions which the peoples of America have once for all embraced and undertaken to defend.

I do not mean to say that any American government would throw any obstacle in the way of any terms of peace the governments now at war might agree upon, or seek to upset them when made, whatever they might be. I only take it for granted that mere terms of peace between the belligerents will not satisfy even the belligerents themselves. Mere agreements may not make peace secure. It will be absolutely necessary that a force be created as a guarantor of the permanency of the settlement so much greater than the force of any nation now engaged or any alliance hitherto formed or projected that no nation, no probable combination of nations could face or withstand it. If the peace presently to be made is to endure, it must be a peace made secure by the organized major force of mankind.

The terms of the immediate peace agreed upon will determine whether it is a peace for which such a guarantee can be secured. The question upon which the whole future peace and policy of the world depends is this: Is the present war a struggle for a just and secure peace, or only for a new balance of power? If it be only a struggle for a new balance of power, who will guarantee, who can guarantee the stable equilibrium of the new arrangement? Only a tranquil Europe can be a stable Europe. There must be, not a balance of power, but a community of power; not organized rivalries, but an organized common peace.

Fortunately we have received very explicit assurances on this point. The statesmen of both of the groups of nations now arrayed against one another have said, in terms that could not be misinterpreted, that it was no part of the purpose they had in mind to crush their antagonists. But the implications of these assurances may not be equally clear to all—may not be the same on both sides of the water. I think it will be serviceable if I attempt to set forth what we understand them to be.

They imply, first of all, that it must be a peace without victory. It is not pleasant to say this. I beg that I may be permitted to put my own interpretation upon it and that it may be understood that no other interpretation was in my thought. I am seeking only to face realities and to face them without soft concealments. Victory would mean peace forced upon the loser, a victor's terms imposed upon the vanquished. It would be accepted in humiliation, under duress, at an intolerable sacrifice, and would leave a sting, a resentment, a bitter memory upon which terms of peace would rest, not permanently, but only as upon quicksand. Only a peace between equals can last. Only a peace the very principle of which is equality and a common participation in a common benefit. The right state of mind, the right feeling between nations, is as necessary for a lasting peace as is the just settlement of vexed questions of territory or of racial and national allegiance.

2. WOODROW WILSON: THE AIMS OF THE WAR AGAINST GERMANY

The United States was not destined to play the role of a neutral mediator because, on January 31, 1917, the German government announced its intention to wage unrestricted submarine warfare. President Wilson responded immediately by severing diplomatic relations with Germany, and pursuing a policy of "armed neutrality." At the same time, American public opinion was outraged

From Ray Stannard Baker and William E. Dodd, eds., *The Public Papers of Woodrow Wilson*, Vol. 5, pp. 8–9, 11–14. Cprt. Edith B. Wilson, 1926.

*by the publication of a secret note from the German Foreign
Minister, Zimmerman, to the German Minister to Mexico, which
had been intercepted by the British. In this note, Zimmerman had
instructed the German Minister in Mexico City that, in the event
of war between Germany and the United States, he should seek a
military alliance with Mexico on the basis of an understanding
that Mexico would regain Texas. In the next few weeks, the sinking of three American merchantmen finally brought President
Wilson to his decision to go to war. The selection below is a major
portion of Wilson's message, delivered to a joint session of Congress on April 2, 1917, in which he asked for a declaration of war
against Germany. Read the selection with care and try to answer
the following questions:*

1. What does Wilson say about our national self-interest when he explains
   the necessity for going to war?
2. What considerations beyond self-interest does he emphasize as appro-
   priate war aims for the American people?

. . . When I addressed the Congress on the twenty-sixth of
February last I thought that it would suffice to assert our neutral rights with arms, our right to use the seas against unlawful
interference, our right to keep our people safe against unlawful
violence. But armed neutrality, it now appears, is impracticable.
Because submarines are in effect outlaws when used as the German submarines have been used against merchant shipping, it is
impossible to defend ships against their attacks as the law of
nations has assumed that merchantmen would defend themselves
against privateers or cruisers, visible craft giving chase upon the
open sea. It is common prudence in such circumstances, grim
necessity indeed, to endeavor to destroy them before they have
shown their own intention. They must be dealt with upon sight,
if dealt with at all. The German Government denies the right of
neutrals to use arms at all within the areas of the sea which it has
proscribed, even in the defense of rights which no modern publi-
cist has ever before questioned their right to defend. The intima-

tion is conveyed that the armed guards which we have placed on our merchant ships will be treated as beyond the pale of law and subject to be dealt with as pirates would be. Armed neutrality is ineffectual enough at best; in such circumstances and in the face of such pretensions it is worse than ineffectual: it is likely only to produce what it was meant to prevent; it is practically certain to draw us into the war without either the rights or the effectiveness of belligerents. There is one choice we cannot make, we are incapable of making: we will not choose the path of submission and suffer the most sacred rights of our Nation and our people to be ignored or violated. The wrongs against which we now array ourselves are no common wrongs; they cut to the very roots of human life.

With a profound sense of the solemn and even tragical character of the step I am taking and of the grave responsibilities which it involves, but in unhesitating obedience to what I deem my constitutional duty, I advise that the Congress declare the recent course of the Imperial German Government to be in fact nothing less than war against the government and people of the United States; that it formally accept the status of belligerent which has thus been thrust upon it; and that it take immediate steps not only to put the country in a more thorough state of defense but also to exert all its power and employ all its resources to bring the Government of the German Empire to terms and end the war. . . .

While we do these things, these deeply momentous things, let us be very clear, and make very clear to all the world what our motives and our objects are. My own thought has not been driven from its habitual and normal course by the unhappy events of the last two months, and I do not believe that the thought of the Nation has been altered or clouded by them. I have exactly the same things in mind now that I had in mind when I addressed the Senate on the twenty-second of January last; the same that I had in mind when I addressed the Congress on the third of February and on the twenty-sixth of February. Our object now, as then, is to vindicate the principles of peace and justice in the no material compensation for the sacrifices we shall freely make. We are but one of the champions of the rights of mankind. We shall be satisfied when those rights have been made as secure as the faith and the freedom of nations can make them.

3. WOODROW WILSON: A FOURTEEN POINT PROGRAM FOR PEACE

the midst of the tremendous tasks that had to be undertaken mobilize American manpower and industry for war, Wilson d every opportunity to express his ideas for a liberal peace to American people and to the people of the world. In Novem-, 1917, the Allied cause suffered a severe blow when the Bol-ik Revolution in Russia was followed by the decision of the leaders of the Russian government to seek a separate peace Germany. The Bolshevik leaders made public all of the t treaties between Russia and the Allies which they found e Czar's archives, and they appealed to the Allies to make a on the basis of no annexations and no indemnities. Wilson l the opportunity to offer a peace program that would coun-Bolshevik propaganda and that would rally the war-weary e of western Europe to make a final effort to win victory. uary 8, 1918, President Wilson delivered, to a joint session gress, an address in which he outlined his famous fourteen rogram for peace. Read the following selection taken from dress, and consider these questions:

new method of diplomacy does Wilson advocate?
economic principles does he think should guide the conduct of ons?
ideas does he propose concerning European colonialism?
eneral principle seems to form the basis of his specific proposals ing political and territorial arrangements in Europe and the Near

nnard Baker and William E. Dodd, eds., *The Public Papers of Woodrow* , pp. 158–161. Cprt. Edith B. Wilson, 1926.

life of the world as against selfish and autocratic power and to set up amongst the really free and self-governed peoples of the world such a concert of purpose and of action as will hence-forth insure the observance of those principles. Neutrality is no longer feasible or desirable where the peace of the world is involved and the freedom of its peoples, and the menace to that peace and freedom lies in the existence of autocratic governments backed by organized force which is controlled wholly by their will, not by the will of their people. We have seen the last of neutrality in such circumstances. We are at the beginning of an age in which it will be insisted that the same standards of conduct and of responsibility for wrong done shall be observed among nations and their governments that are observed among the individual citizens of civilized states.

We have no quarrel with the German people. We have no feeling towards them but one of sympathy and friendship. It was not upon their impulse that their government acted in entering this war. It was not with their previous knowledge or approval. It was a war determined upon as wars used to be determined upon in the old, unhappy days when peoples were nowhere consulted by their rulers and wars were provoked and waged in the interest of dynasties or of little groups of ambitious men who were accustomed to use their fellow men as pawns and tools. Self-governed nations do not fill their neighbor states with spies or set the course of intrigue to bring about some critical posture of affairs which will give them an opportunity to strike and make conquest. Such designs can be successfully worked out only under cover and where no one has the right to ask questions. Cunningly contrived plans of deception or aggression, carried, it may be, from generation to generation, can be worked out and kept from the light only within the privacy of courts or behind the carefully guarded confidences of a narrow and privileged class. They are happily impossible where public opinion commands and insists upon full information concerning all the nation's affairs.

A steadfast concert for peace can never be maintained except by a partnership of democratic nations. No autocratic government could be trusted to keep faith within it or observe its covenants. It must be a league of honor, a partnership of opinion. Intrigue would eat its vitals away; the plottings of inner circles who could plan what they would and render account to no one would be a corruption seated at its very heart. Only free peoples can hold their purpose and their honor steady to a common end and prefer the interests of mankind to any narrow interest of their own.

Does not every American feel that assurance has been added to our hope for the future peace of the world by the wonderful and heartening things that have been happening within the last few weeks in Russia?* Russia was known by those who knew it best to have been always in fact democratic at heart, in all the vital habits of her thought, in all the intimate relationships of her people that spoke their natural instinct, their habitual attitude towards life. The autocracy that crowned the summit of her political structure, long as it had stood and terrible as was the reality of its power, was not in fact Russian in origin, character, or purpose; and now it has been shaken off and the great, generous Russian people have been added in all their naive majesty and might to the forces that are fighting for freedom in the world, for justice, and for peace. Here is a fit partner for a League of Honor.

One of the things that has served to convince us that the Prussian autocracy was not and could never be our friend is that from the very outset of the present war it has filled our unsuspecting communities and even our offices of government with spies and set criminal intrigues everywhere afoot against our national unity of counsel, our peace within and without, our industries and our commerce. Indeed, it is now evident that its spies were here even before the war began; and it is unhappily not a matter

---

* Wilson is referring to the first stage of the Russian Revolution in 1917, before the Bolsheviks seized power.—Ed.

---

of conjecture but a fact proved in our courts of justice th intrigues which have more than once come perilously n disturbing the peace and dislocating the industries of th try have been carried on at the instigation, with the supp even under the personal direction of official agents of perial Government accredited to the Government of th States. Even in checking these things and trying to them we have sought to put the most generous int possible upon them because we knew that their sou in any hostile feeling or purpose of the German peo us (who were no doubt as ignorant of them as were), but only in the selfish designs of a Governr what it pleased and told its people nothing. But the their part in serving to convince us at last that tha entertains no real friendship for us and means to peace and security at its convenience. That it m enemies against us at our very doors the interce German Minister at Mexico City is eloquent ev

We are accepting this challenge of hostile pu know that in such a Government, following can never have a friend; and that in the pre ized power, always lying in wait to accomplish purpose, there can be no assured security Governments of the world. We are now abo battle with this natural foe to liberty an spend the whole force of the Nation to che tensions and its power. We are glad, now with no veil of false pretense about ther ultimate peace of the world and for the the German peoples included: for the ri small and the privilege of men everywl of life and of obedience. The world m mocracy. Its peace must be planted upc political liberty. We have no selfish e conquest, no dominion. We seek n

5. According to Wilson, how should a peace built on such principles be guaranteed?

. . . It will be our wish and purpose that the processes of peace, when they are begun, shall be absolutely open and that they shall involve and permit henceforth no secret understandings of any kind. The day of conquest and aggrandizement is gone by; so is also the day of secret covenants entered into in the interest of particular governments and likely at some unlooked-for moment to upset the peace of the world. It is this happy fact, now clear to the view of every public man whose thoughts do not still linger in an age that is dead and gone, which makes it possible for every nation whose purposes are consistent with justice and the peace of the world to avow now or at any other time the objects it has in view.

We entered this war because violations of right had occurred which touched us to the quick and made the life of our own people impossible unless they were corrected and the world secured once for all against their recurrence. What we demand in this war, therefore, is nothing peculiar to ourselves. It is that the world be made fit and safe to live in; and particularly that it be made safe for every peace-loving nation which, like our own, wishes to live its own life, determine its own institutions, be assured of justice and fair dealing by the other peoples of the world as against force and selfish aggression. All the peoples of the world are in effect partners in this interest, and for our own part we see very clearly that unless justice be done to others it will not be done to us. The program of the world's peace, therefore, is our program; and that program, the only possible program, as we see it, is this:

I. Open covenants of peace, openly arrived at, after which there shall be no private international understandings of any kind but diplomacy shall proceed always frankly and in the public view.

II. Absolute freedom of navigation upon the seas, outside territorial waters, alike in peace and in war, except as the seas may be closed in whole or in part by international action for the enforcement of international covenants.

III. The removal, so far as possible, of all economic barriers and the establishment of an equality of trade conditions among all the nations consenting to the peace and associating themselves for its maintenance.

IV. Adequate guarantees given and taken that national armaments will be reduced to the lowest point consistent with domestic safety.

V. A free, open-minded, and absolutely impartial adjustment of all colonial claims, based upon a strict observance of the principle that in determining all such questions of sovereignty the interests of the populations concerned must have equal weight with the equitable claims of the government whose title is to be determined.

VI. The evacuation of all Russian territory and such a settlement of all questions affecting Russia as will secure the best and freest cooperation of the other nations of the world in obtaining for her an unhampered and unembarrassed opportunity for the independent determination of her own political development and national policy and assure her of a sincere welcome into the society of free nations under institutions of her own choosing; and, more than a welcome, assistance also of every kind that she may need and may herself desire. The treatment accorded Russia by her sister nations in the months to come will be the acid test of their good will, of their comprehension of her needs as distinguished from their own interests, and of their intelligent and unselfish sympathy.

VII. Belgium, the whole world will agree, must be evacuated and restored, without any attempt to limit the sovereignty which she enjoys in common with all other free nations. No other single act will serve as this will serve to restore confidence among the nations in the laws which they have themselves set and determined for the government of their relations with one another. Without this healing act the whole structure and validity of international law is forever impaired.

VIII. All French territory should be freed and the invaded portions restored, and the wrong done to France by Prussia in 1871 in the matter of Alsace-Lorraine, which has unsettled the peace of the world for nearly fifty years, should be righted, in order that peace may once more be made secure in the interest of all.

IX. A readjustment of the frontiers of Italy should be effected along clearly recognizable lines of nationality.

X. The peoples of Austria-Hungary, whose place among the nations we wish to see safeguarded and assured, should be accorded the freest opportunity of autonomous development.

XI. Rumania, Serbia, and Montenegro should be evacuated; occupied territories restored; Serbia accorded free and secure access to the sea; and the relations of the several Balkan states to one another determined by friendly counsel along historically established lines of allegiance and nationality; and international guarantees of the political and economic independence and territorial integrity of the several Balkan states should be entered into.

XII. The Turkish portions of the present Ottoman Empire should be assured a secure sovereignty, but the other nationalities which are now under Turkish rule should be assured an undoubted security of life and an absolutely unmolested opportunity of autonomous development, and the Dardanelles should be permanently opened as a free passage to the ships and commerce of all nations under international guarantees.

XIII. An independent Polish state should be erected which should include the territories inhabited by indisputably Polish populations, which should be assured a free and secure access to the sea, and whose political and economic independence and territorial integrity should be guaranteed by international covenant.

XIV. A general association of nations must be formed under

specific covenants for the purpose of affording mutual guarantees of political independence and territorial integrity to great and small states alike.

In regard to these essential rectifications of wrong and assertions of right we feel ourselves to be intimate partners of all the governments and peoples associated together against the Imperialists. We cannot be separated in interest or divided in purpose. We stand together until the end.

4. Woodrow Wilson: The Treaty and The Covenant

Although the leaders of the Allied Governments in Europe were not ready to abandon their principles of diplomacy based on considerations of national self-interest and the balance of power, Wilson's "Fourteen Points" had a tremendous impact upon public opinion in Europe. When the German armies were driven back to the German frontier by the Allied offensive in the autumn of 1918, the German government appealed for an armistice on the basis of the Fourteen Points. And when the Peace Conference met in Paris, the Fourteen Points became the basis of Wilson's daily battles with other Allied leaders in the negotiations for a peace settlement. In the final outcome, Wilson had to make many concessions to the demands of other Allied leaders that compromised some of his principles, but he did win agreement on the establishment of an international organization—the League of Nations—to guarantee the peace and to adjust future grievances that might lead to war. The following selection is taken from Wilson's address to the Senate of the United States, on July 10, 1919, in which he laid the Treaty and the League Covenant before that body for ratification. Read the selection carefully and try to answer these questions:

From Ray Stannard Baker and William E. Dodd, eds., *The Public Papers of Woodrow Wilson*, Vol. 5, pp. 542–549. Cprt. Edith B. Wilson, 1926.

1. Why, in his opinion, has the League of Nations become "an indispensable instrumentality" and "the only hope for mankind"?
2. How does Wilson explain the compromises of his peace-making principles? What difficult and practical questions made such compromises necessary?

. . . The atmosphere in which the Conference worked seemed created, not by the ambitions of strong governments, but by the hopes and aspirations of small nations and of peoples hitherto under bondage to the power that victory had shattered and destroyed. Two great empires had been forced into political bankruptcy, and we were the receivers. Our task was not only to make peace with the Central Empires and remedy the wrongs their armies had done. The Central Empires had lived in open violation of many of the very rights for which the war had been fought, dominating alien peoples over whom they had no natural right to rule, enforcing, not obedience, but veritable bondage, exploiting those who were weak for the benefit of those who were masters and overlords only by force of arms. There could be no peace until the whole order of Central Europe was set right.

That meant that new nations were to be created,—Poland, Czecho-Slovakia, Hungary itself. No part of ancient Poland had ever in any true sense become a part of Germany, or of Austria, or of Russia. Bohemia was alien in every thought and hope to the monarchy of which she had so long been an artificial part; and the uneasy partnership between Austria and Hungary had been one rather of interest than of kinship or sympathy. The Slavs whom Austria had chosen to force into her empire on the south were kept to their obedience by nothing but fear. Their hearts were with their kinsmen in the Balkans. These were all arrangements of power, not arrangements of natural union or association. It was the imperative task of those who would make peace and make it intelligently to establish a new order which would rest upon the free choice of peoples rather than upon the arbitrary authority of Hapsburgs or Hohenzollerns.

More than that, great populations bound by sympathy and actual kin to Rumania were also linked against their will to the conglomerate Austro-Hungarian monarchy or to other alien sovereignties, and it was part of the task of peace to make a new Rumania as well as a new slavic state clustering about Serbia.

And no natural frontiers could be found to these new fields of adjustment and redemption. It was necessary to look constantly forward to other related tasks. The German colonies were to be disposed of. They had not been governed; they had been exploited merely, without thought of the interest or even the ordinary human rights of their inhabitants.

The Turkish Empire, moreover, had fallen apart, as the Austro-Hungarian had. It had never had any real unity. It had been held together only by pitiless, inhuman force. Its peoples cried aloud for release, for succor from unspeakable distress, for all that the new day of hope seemed at last to bring within its dawn. Peoples hitherto in utter darkness were to be led out into the same light and given at last a helping hand. Undeveloped peoples and peoples ready for recognition but not yet ready to assume the full responsibilities of statehood were to be given adequate guarantees of friendly protection, guidance and assistance.

And out of the execution of these great enterprises of liberty sprang opportunities to attempt what statesmen had never found the way before to do; an opportunity to throw safeguards about the rights of racial, national and religious minorities by solemn international covenant; an opportunity to limit and regulate military establishments where they were most likely to be mischievous; an opportunity to effect a complete and systematic internationalization of waterways and railways which were necessary to the free economic life of more than one nation and to clear many of the normal channels of commerce of unfair obstructions of law or of privilege; and the very welcome opportunity to secure for labor the concerted protection of definite international pledges of principle and practice.

These were not tasks which the Conference looked about it

to find and went out of its way to perform. They were insepa-
rable from the settlements of peace. They were thrust upon it by
circumstances which could not be overlooked. The war had
created them. In all quarters of the world old-established relationships had been disturbed or broken and affairs were at loose
ends, needing to be mended or united again, but could not be
made what they were before. They had to be set right by apply-
ing some uniform principle of justice or enlightened expediency.
And they could not be adjusted by merely prescribing in a treaty
what should be done. New states were to be set up which could
not hope to live through their first period of weakness without
assured support by the great nations that had consented to their
creation and won for them their independence. Ill-governed colonies could not be put in the hands of governments which were
to act as trustees for their people and not as their masters if there
was to be no common authority among the nations to which they
were to be responsible in the execution of their trust. Future international conventions with regard to the control of waterways,
with regard to illicit traffic of many kinds, in arms or in deadly
drugs, or with regard to the adjustment of many varying international administrative arrangements could not be assured if the
treaty were to provide no permanent common international
agency, if its execution in such matters was to be left to the
slow and uncertain processes of cooperation by ordinary methods of negotiation. . . . A league of free nations had become a
practical necessity. Examine the treaty of peace and you will
find that everywhere throughout its manifold provisions its fram-
ers have felt obliged to turn to the League of Nations as an indispensable instrumentality for the maintenance of the new order
it has been their purpose to set up in the world,—the world of
civilized men.

That there should be a League of Nations to steady the counsels and maintain the peaceful understandings of the world, to
make, not treaties alone, but the accepted principles of international law as well, the actual rule of conduct among the gov-

ernments of the world, had been one of the agreements accepted from the first as the basis of peace with the Central Powers. The statesmen of all the belligerent countries were agreed that such a league must be created to sustain the settlements that were to be effected. But at first I think there was a feeling among some of them that, while it must be attempted, the formation of such a league was perhaps a counsel of perfection which practical men, long experienced in the world of affairs, must agree to very cautiously and with many misgivings. It was only as the difficult work of arranging an all but universal adjustment of the world's affairs advanced from day to day from one stage of conference to another that it became evident to them that what they were seeking would be little more than something written upon paper, to be interpreted and applied by such methods as the chances of politics might make available if they did not provide a means of common counsel which all were obliged to accept, a common authority whose decisions would be recognized as decisions which all must respect.

And so the most practical, the most skeptical among them turned more and more to the League as the authority through which international action was to be secured, the authority without which, as they had come to see it, it would be difficult to give assured effect either to this treaty or to any other international understanding upon which they were to depend for the maintenance of peace. The fact that the Covenant of the League was the first substantive part of the treaty to be worked out and agreed upon, while all else was in solution, helped to make the formulation of the rest easier. The Conference was, after all, not to be ephemeral. The concert of nations was to continue, under a definite Covenant which had been agreed upon and which all were convinced was workable. They could go forward with confidence to make arrangements intended to be permanent. The most practical of the conferees were at last the most ready to refer to the League of Nations the superintendence of all interests which did not admit of immediate determination, of all administrative problems which were to require a continuing over-sight. What had seemed a counsel of perfection had come to seem a plain counsel of necessity. The League of Nations was the practical statesman's hope of success in many of the most difficult things he was attempting.

And it had validated itself in the thought of every member of the Conference as something much bigger, much greater every way, than a mere instrument for carrying out the provisions of a particular treaty. It was universally recognized that all the peoples of the world demanded of the Conference that it should create such a continuing concert of free nations as would make wars of aggression and spoliation such as this that has just ended forever impossible. A cry had gone out from every home in every stricken land from which sons and brothers and fathers had gone forth to the great sacrifice that such a sacrifice should never again be exacted. It was manifest why it had been exacted. It had been exacted because one nation desired dominion and other nations had known no means of defense except armaments and alliances. War had lain at the heart of every arrangement of the Europe,— of every arrangement of the world,—that preceded the war. Restive peoples had been told that fleets and armies, which they toiled to sustain, meant peace; and they now knew that they had been lied to: that fleets and armies had been maintained to promote national ambitions and meant war. They knew that no old policy meant anything else but force, force,—always force. And they knew that it was intolerable. Every true heart in the world, and every enlightened judgment demanded that, at whatever cost of independent action, every government that took thought for its people or for justice or for ordered freedom should lend itself to a new purpose and utterly destroy the old order of international politics. Statesmen might see difficulties, but the people could see none and could brook no denial. A war in which they had been bled white to beat the terror that lay concealed in every Balance of Power must not end in a mere victory of arms and a new balance. The monster that had resorted to arms must be put in chains that could not be broken. The united power of free nations must put a stop to aggression, and the world must be given peace. If there was not the will or the intelligence to accomplish that now, there must be another and a final war and the world must be swept clean of every power that could renew the terror. The League of Nations was not merely an instrument to adjust and remedy old wrongs under a new treaty of peace; it was the only hope for mankind. Again and again had the demon of war been cast out of the house of the peoples and the house swept clean by a treaty of peace; only to prepare a time when he would enter in again with spirits worse than himself. The house must now be given a tenant who could hold it against all such. Convenient, indeed indispensable, as statesmen found the newly planned League of Nations to be for the execution of present plans of peace and reparation, they saw it in a new aspect before their work was finished. They saw it as the main object of the peace, as the only thing that could complete it or make it worth while. They saw it as the hope of the world, and that hope they did not dare to disappoint. Shall we or any other free people hesitate to accept this great duty? . . .

And so the result of the Conference of Peace, so far as Germany is concerned, stands complete. The difficulties encountered were very many. Sometimes they seemed insuperable. It was impossible to accommodate the interests of so great a body of nations,—interests which directly or indirectly affected almost every nation in the world,—without many minor compromises. The treaty, as a result, is not exactly what we would have written. It is probably not what any one of the national delegations would have written. But results were worked out which on the whole bear test. I think that it will be found that the compromises which were accepted as inevitable nowhere cut to the heart of any principle. The work of the Conference squares, as a whole, with the principles agreed upon as the basis of the peace as well as with the practical possibilities of the international situations which had to be faced and dealt with as facts.

In this part of our inquiry, we shall examine several documents which reveal the conceptions of peacemaking that were developed by leaders in the United States and Europe who did not agree with Wilson's thinking. One of these selections, written by Theodore Roosevelt, represents the belief, shared by Henry Cabot Lodge and other senators, that national interests should come first in any peace settlement. The other four selections represent a similar emphasis in the thinking of European leaders. In particular, they will enable us to see how the two leading Allied Powers, Britain and France, sought a peace settlement that would make concessions to their long-established conceptions of national self-interest. To help you understand these documents better, a brief summary of the historical background of European diplomacy has been included as the first selection in this part of your readings.

Part 3

The Diplomacy of Self-Interest

5. THE PATTERN OF OLD WORLD DIPLOMACY: A SUMMARY

MUCH of Woodrow Wilson's thinking about a just and desirable peace represented a rejection of the system of international politics that had developed before 1914. In the decades before the outbreak of the war, explosive pressures had been built up by imperialist rivalries, the suppression of national minorities, and a diplomacy which was based upon military alliances and an uncertain balance of power.

Beginning in the 1880's there was a wholesale scramble for colonial dominion among the more powerful nations of the world. Much of the African continent was divided among various European nations. The larger shares went to Britain and France: the British were dominant in the south and the east, while the French occupied much of the north and west including nearly the whole Sahara desert. The Germans and the Italians, who were latecomers in the colonial game, picked up relatively unprofitable lands, but the Belgians were able to acquire the potentially rich area of the Congo through the efforts of a business-minded king. Spain and Portugal also held areas which had been taken over in an earlier age of exploration and discovery.

Furthermore, the leading European powers were wresting important economic concessions and extra-territorial privileges from the Chinese Empire; while Japan, rapidly modernizing itself, began its penetration of Korea and Manchuria. The United States gained a colonial empire with the acquisition of the Philippine Islands, Guam, and Puerto Rico, and pursued, in addition, an aggressive policy of intervention in the affairs of Latin America republics in the Caribbean area.

The tensions created around the world by colonialism and imperialism were accompanied by the explosive pressure of the nationalities problem in Europe. In central and eastern Europe, the great inland empires—Germany, Austria-Hungary, and Russia—contained many national minorities that aspired to some kind of independent existence. In the Russian Empire, the national minorities that were most restless were the Finns, the small Baltic peoples, and especially the Poles. The polyglot Austro-Hungarian empire included Poles, Czechs, Slovaks, Rumanians, Serbs, Croats, and Slovenes who yearned for deliverance from their status as subject peoples. Germany, too, had its minority problems—with the provinces of Alsace and Lorraine, wrested from France in 1870, and with the Poles who inhabited the eastern lands which linked East Prussia with Germany across the lower reaches of the Vistula River.

These minority problems were aggravated by the cross-pressures of expansionist ambitions that were expressed in the so-called "Pan" movements. This type of continental imperialism was based upon ideologies that taught the superiority of one's own linguistic group. Thus, a vigorous Pan-Slav movement in Russia encouraged many other Slavic peoples in Eastern Europe to look to Russia for deliverance from their German or Hungarian rulers. Pan-Germanism looked toward the uniting of all Germanic dynasties in Central and Eastern Europe into an effective alliance of ruling groups which could dominate the political and cultural development of the area. The success of Pan-Germanism could only be achieved by the defeat of Pan-Slavism, and vice versa. Hence both movements tended to breed intolerant and jingoistic attitudes.

The many conflicts of interest among the great powers shaped European diplomacy toward the creation of a system of alliances that would provide some degree of military security. Germany and Austria-Hungary were bound together by close dynastic and political ties, and Italy was joined to Germany in a defensive military pact. Russia and France signed a military agreement in 1894; and the British, alarmed by their isolation among the great powers during the Boer War, reached a "cordial understanding" with France in 1904. In 1907, this became a "Triple Entente" when Britain and Russia achieved a settlement of past differences. The rivalry between the "Triple Alliance" and the "Triple Entente" encouraged a notable increase of popular militarism in all countries, as well as a dangerous naval race between Britain and Germany.

When the chips were down in 1914, the Triple Entente held together more successfully than the Triple Alliance. After the assassination of the Archduke Francis Ferdinand at Sarajevo by a young Serbian nationalist, Austria-Hungary sent a threatening ultimatum to Serbia. Thereupon Russia supported Serbia, Germany supported Austria, France supported Russia, and Britain supported France; only Italy remained aloof from the rapidly spreading chain of ultimatums and military mobilizations. On August 4, 1914, the armies started to move and, with the booming guns of August, Europe was plunged into the holocaust of a general war.

Furthermore, even when the illusions of a brief war and quick victories, so widely shared by the leaders of the warring nations in August of 1914, were shattered by the nightmare of deadlocked trench warfare and millions of casualties, the old patterns of diplomacy continued to prevail. In 1914, Bulgaria was enticed into the war on the side of the Central Powers with the promise of extensive territorial gains at Serbia's expense. In 1915, Italy was brought into the war on the side of the Allied Powers by means of the secret Treaty of London, which promised to give Italy stretches of Austrian territory and further acquisitions at the expense of Turkey. Rumania chose to enter the war in 1916, at what seemed to be a favorable moment to seize a large part of Transylvania from the hard-pressed Hungarians. Greece finally joined the Allied Powers early in 1917, counting on their promises of support for future annexations at the expense of Turkey and Bulgaria.

Accordingly, the willingness of the great powers to continue the war in the face of the staggering casualties of the Western and Eastern fronts was nourished by their long-cherished ambitions. Germany continued to hope for the decisive victories that would enable her to achieve the political hegemony that German leaders had dreamed about. England accepted the terrible human sacrifices as a necessary means to eliminate German naval and colonial rivalry. France poured out its blood to redeem the lost province of Alsace and Lorraine, and Russia pursued its age-old goal of controlling the Dardanelles. These French, British and Russian aims were also embodied in secret treaties.

Thus, the nations of the Old World were still controlled by ancient ambitions and hard-headed calculations of national interests. Their leaders, therefore, were bound to differ with Woodrow Wilson about the peace settlement.

6. THEODORE ROOSEVELT: "THE LEAGUE OF NATIONS"

The United States had clearly emerged as a world power in the Spanish American War of 1898, but not until Theodore Roosevelt succeeded to the Presidency did we have a Chief Executive who understood some of the responsibilities of America's new position in international politics. He encouraged the development of a strong navy to protect America's far-flung interests; in addition he developed a vigorous foreign policy in the Far East and the Caribbean. His years in the White House also made him aware of the delicate and uncertain balance of power that existed in Europe. Consequently, when war broke out in Europe in 1914, Theodore Roosevelt perceived immediately that America's strategic interests were roughly parallel to those of France and England. He began to attack President Wilson's negotiations with Germany concerning the problem of submarine warfare as cowardly and pusillanimous. Indeed, he was among the first to lead a campaign for military preparedness in the event that we were drawn into the war. After the United States entered the war, Theodore Roosevelt became one of the recognized leaders of the opposition to Wilson's peace program. The following selection is an editorial written by Theodore Roosevelt for the Kansas City Star *in November, 1918, shortly after the Armistice had ended the fighting in Europe. As you read it, consider the following questions:*

From the *Kansas City Star*, November 17, 1918. Reprinted with permission.

1. What kind of a League of Nations is Roosevelt willing to support?
2. What nations would he include in a League and which would he exclude?
3. What are the two most menacing dangers in the world as he sees them?
4. Does Roosevelt want to do away with the division of the world into "spheres of interest"?
5. Do you think that the international organization that he proposed would be more like a military alliance than a League of Nations?

There are so many prior things to do and so much uncertainty as to the form of agreement for permanently increasing the chances of peace that it is difficult to do more than make a general statement as to what is desirable and possibly feasible in the league of nations plan. It would certainly be folly to discuss it overmuch until some of the existing obstacles to peace are overcome. That such discussion may be not futile, but mischievous, has been vividly shown in the last six weeks. During the first week of October President Wilson and Germany agreed on the famous fourteen points of Mr. Wilson's as a basis for peace. But this agreement amounted to nothing whatever except for a moment it gave Germany the hope that she could escape disaster by a negotiated peace. The emphatic protest of our own people caused this hope to vanish, and just five weeks later peace came, not on Mr. Wilson's fourteen points, but on General Foch's twenty-odd points, which had all the directness, the straightforwardness, and the unequivocal clearness which the fourteen points strikingly lacked.*

Nevertheless, it is well to begin considering now the things which we think can be done and the things that we think cannot be done in making a league of nations. In the first place, we ought to realize that the population of the world clearly understands that in this war they have been involved to a degree never

---

* Roosevelt is referring to the conditions for an armistice that General Foch, the Commander-in-Chief of the Allied Armies, imposed upon the German General Staff.—Ed.

hitherto known. In consequence the horror of the war is very real, and people are at least thinking of the need of cooperation with much greater fixity of purpose and of understanding than ever before. Of course, fundamentally war and peace are matters of the heart rather than of organization, and any declaration or peace league which represents the high-flown sentimentality of pacifists and doctrinaires will be worse than useless; but if, without in the smallest degree sacrificing our belief in a sound and intense national aim, we all join with the people of England, France, and Italy and with the people in smaller states who in practice show themselves able to steer equally clear of Bolshevism and of Kaiserism, we may be able to make a real and much-needed advance in the international organization. The United States cannot again completely withdraw into its shell. We need not mix in all European quarrels nor assume all spheres of interest everywhere to be ours, but we ought to join with the other civilized nations of the world in some scheme that in a time of great stress would offer a likelihood of obtaining just settlements that will avert war.

Therefore, in my judgment, the United States at the peace conference ought to be able to cooperate effectively with the British and French and Italian Governments to support a practical and effective plan which won't attempt the impossible, but which will represent a real step forward.

Probably the first essential would be to limit the league at the outset to the Allies, to the peoples with whom we have been operating and with whom we are certain we can cooperate in the future. Neither Turkey nor Austria need now be considered as regards such a league, and we should clearly understand that Bolshevist Russia is, and that Bolshevist Germany would be, as undesirable in such a league as the Germany and Russia of the Hohenzollerns and Romanoffs. Bolshevism is just as much an international menace as Kaiserism. Until Germany and Russia have proved by a course of conduct extending over years that they are capable of entering such a league in good faith, so that we can count upon their fulfilling their duties in it, it would be merely foolish to take them in.

The league, therefore, would have to be based on the combination among the Allies of the present war—together with any peoples like Czecho-Slovaks, who have shown that they are fully entitled to enter into such a league if they desire to do so. Each nation should absolutely reserve to itself its right to establish its own tariff and general economic policy, and absolutely ought to control such vital questions as immigration and citizenship and the form of government it prefers. Then it would probably be best for certain spheres of interest to be reserved to each nation or a group of nations.

The northernmost portion of South America and Mexico and Central America, all of them fronting on the Panama Canal, have a special interest to the United States, more interest than they can have for any European or Asiatic power. The general conduct of Eastern Asiatic policy bears a most close relationship to Japan. The same thing is true as regards other nations and certain of the peculiarly African and European questions. Everything outside of what is thus reserved, which affects any two members of the league or affects one member of the league and outsiders, should be decided by some species of court, and all the people of the league should guarantee to use their whole strength in enforcing the decision.

This, of course, means that all the free peoples must keep reasonably prepared for defense and for helping well-behaved nations against the nations or hordes which represent despotism, barbarism, and anarchy. As far as the United States is concerned, I believe we should keep our navy to the highest possible point of efficiency and have it second in size to that of Great Britain alone, and we should then have universal obligatory military training for all our young men for a period of, say, nine months during some one year between the ages of nineteen and twenty-three inclusive. This would not represent militarism, but an antidote against militarism. It would not represent a great expense. On the contrary, it would mean to give to every citizen of our country an education which would fit him to do his work as a citizen as no other type of education could.

There are some nations with which there would not be the slightest difficulty in going much further than this. The time has now come when it would be perfectly safe to enter into universal arbitration treaties with the British Empire, for example, reserving such rights only as Australia and Canada themselves would reserve inside the British Empire; but there are a number of outside peoples with whom it would not be safe to go much further than above outlined. If we only made this one kind of agreement, we could keep it, and we should make no agreement that we would not and could not keep. More essential than anything else is it for us to remember that in matters of this kind an ounce of practical performance is worth a ton of windy rhetorical promises.

7. ARMISTICE STIPULATIONS OF BRITAIN AND FRANCE

By October 1, 1918, the Allied armies had broken through the Hindenberg Line and were approaching the German frontier. The German government appealed to Woodrow Wilson for an armistice on the basis of the Fourteen Points. Wilson looked upon this as a golden opportunity to establish the proper preconditions for peacemaking, but his European allies refused to accept such moderate terms. After several stormy interviews with Wilson's emissary, Colonel House, the British and French governments agreed to make peace on the basis of the Fourteen Points provided that certain stipulations were added. Read the text of these stipulations carefully and consider the following questions:

From page 71—*The Truth About the Treaty* by André Tardieu, copyright 1921 by the Bobbs-Merrill Company, Inc., 19448 by Julia Angelique Largenten, reprinted by permission of the publishers.

1. The paragraph relating to the question of the "freedom of the seas" was put in at the insistence of the British. Why do you suppose that the British would insist on such a reservation?
2. Why do you suppose that the French government took the lead in insisting on the stipulation concerning compensation for damages?

The Allied Governments have given careful consideration to the correspondence which has passed between the President of the United States and the German Government.

Subject to the qualifications which follow they declare their willingness to make peace with the Government of Germany on the terms of peace laid down in the Address of the President to Congress on January 8, 1918, and the principles of settlement enunciated in his subsequent address.

They must point out, however, that clause 2, relating to what is usually described as the "Freedom of the Seas" is open to various interpretations some of which they could not accept. They must therefore reserve to themselves complete freedom on this subject when they enter the Peace Conference.

Furthermore in the conditions of peace laid down in his address to Congress on January 8, 1918, the President declared that the invaded territories must be restored as well as evacuated and freed and the Allied Governments feel that no doubt ought to be allowed to exist as to what this provision implies. By it they understand that compensations will be made by Germany for all damage done to the civilian population of the Allies and their property by the aggression of Germany by land, by sea and from the air.

8. GEORGES CLEMENCEAU: "THERE ARE OLD WRONGS TO BE RIGHTED"

Georges Clemenceau, the French Prime Minister, had won the nickname of "the Tiger" because of the fighting qualities he had displayed in French politics. Seventy-eight years old at the time of the Peace Conference, he was a member of the generation that had lost the War of 1870 to Germany. Since those bitter days of defeat, he had remained utterly devoted to the restoration of the glory and honor of France, as well as her lost provinces. Furthermore, Clemenceau's experiences in French and European politics had made him hard-boiled and cynical. He was suspicious of high-sounding phrases and could make devastating use of his quick wit to disconcert his opponents. Of Wilson's Fourteen Points he remarked, "The good Lord himself had only ten." The following speech was delivered by Clemenceau to the French Chamber of Deputies on December 30, 1918, when he asked for a vote of confidence on the eve of the Peace Conference. Keep the following questions in mind as you read his remarks:

1. To what "old system" is Clemenceau determined to be faithful?
2. What does he think is the best guarantee of French security?
3. Why does he think that Wilson cannot fully understand the French situation.

. . . Do not forget [he continued] that France is in a peculiarly difficult situation. She is the nearest country to Germany. America is far off, and naturally took some time to come to us. Great Britain came at once at the call of Mr. Asquith, and that is the thing I wanted to say especially to-day. During all this time it is we who have suffered; it was our men who were mown down, our towns and villages that were devastated. It has been said, "This must not occur again." Quite so; but how? There is an old system which appears to be discredited today, but to which I am not afraid of saying I am still faithful. Countries have or-

Reprinted with permission from the London *Times*, December 31, 1918, p. 8.

ganized solidly defended frontiers with the necessary armaments and the balance of Power. This system seems to be condemned by a few high authorities; nevertheless, I should like to point out that, if we had had such a balance of Power before the war, that if the United States, Great Britain, France, and Italy had declared that whoever attacked one of them would have to expect the other three to assume the task of common defence . . . [Clemenceau's words were drowned out by applause at this point].

Here in this system of alliance which I do not give up, it is the thought which will guide me in the conference, if your confidence allows me to be present at it. There must be nothing which can separate in the period after the war the four Great Powers whom the war has united. I shall make every sacrifice to maintain the Entente; but why before beginning the discussion should I develop before you the arguments which I wish to see accepted? . . .

As to international guarantees, I say that if France is left free to organize her own military defence—for she does not wish to be invaded again—if she is mistress of her own military organizations, I shall accept any supplementary guarantee which may be given to me. I go further, and say that if those guarantees are such as will demand sacrifices in the way of military preparation, I shall accept those sacrifices with joy, because I do not wish to see my country suffer without necessity. . . . The truth is that since the most distant ages of history peoples have thrown themselves upon each other in order to satisfy their appetites. . . .

Look at our situation. Do you not think it is good to approach the Conference with authority, if I may use a word which we have acquired in war leadership? People have spoken of the visit President Wilson paid me. He did do me the honor of calling upon me. I made it a principle not to question him, and let him talk to me. He did so. He explained his views, his reasons, and his means of supporting them. It would be a lie if I said that I was in agreement with him on all points. America is far away from Germany; France is quite close to it, and I have concerns which do not affect him as much as they do a man who has seen the Germans in his own country during four years. There are old wrongs to be righted. . . .

9. DAVID LLOYD GEORGE: SOME CONSIDERATIONS FOR THE PEACE CONFERENCE

David Lloyd George, the British Prime Minister, came to the Peace Conference fresh from his victory in the British parliamentary elections held in December of 1918. Wartime emotions were still very high, and Lloyd George had won a landslide victory by advocating the punishment of those who were responsible for the "crime" of plunging Europe into a war that had "sent millions of the best young men of Europe to death and mutilation." At the Peace Conference, however, the British Prime Minister played a cool-headed role in defining and protecting British national interests. With the help of his advisors, he prepared a set of proposals that outlined the kind of a treaty of peace that the British wanted. These proposals were submitted to the Peace Conference on March 25, 1919. Read the text of this memorandum carefully, and try to answer the following questions:

1. Why is Lloyd George willing to strip Germany of its overseas colonies, but unwilling to take away any territories in Europe that include large numbers of German-speaking people?
2. Why is Lloyd George reluctant to place heavy burdens of reparations on Germany or to place permanent limitations on German armaments?
3. What is the great danger to the future peace of Europe that worries him?
4. To reassure France, what guarantees does he propose against the possibility of future German aggression?
5. Is his conception of a League of Nations very different from Wilson's?

From David Lloyd George, *The Truth About the Peace Treaties* (London: Victor Gollancz, Ltd., 1938), pp. 404–416. Reprinted with permission.

I

When nations are exhausted by wars in which they have put forth all their strength and which leave them tired, bleeding and broken, it is not difficult to patch up a peace that may last until the generation which experienced the horrors of the war has passed away. Pictures of heroism and triumph only tempt those who know nothing of the sufferings and terrors of war. It is therefore comparatively easy to patch up a peace which will last for thirty years.

What is difficult, however, is to draw up a peace which will not provoke a fresh struggle when those who have had practical experience of what war means have passed away. History has proved that a peace, which has been hailed by a victorious nation as a triumph of diplomatic skill and statesmanship, even of moderation in the long run, has proved itself to be shortsighted and charged with danger to the victor. The peace of 1871 was believed by Germany to ensure not only her security but her permanent supremacy. The facts have shown exactly the contrary. France itself has demonstrated that those who say you can make Germany so feeble that she will never be able to hit back are utterly wrong. Year by year France became numerically weaker in comparison with her victorious neighbour, but in reality she became ever more powerful. She kept watch on Europe; she made alliances with those whom Germany had wronged or menaced; she never ceased to warn the world of its danger and ultimately she was able to secure the overthrow of the far mightier power which had trampled so brutally upon her. You may strip Germany of her colonies, reduce her armaments to a mere police force and her navy to that of a fifth-rate power; all the same in the end if she feels that she has been unjustly treated in the peace of 1919 she will find means of exacting retribution from her conquerors. The impression, the deep impression, made upon the human heart by four years of unexampled slaughter will disappear with the hearts upon which it has been marked by the terrible sword of the great war. The maintenance of peace will then depend upon there being no causes of exasperation constantly stirring up the spirit of patriotism, of justice or of fairplay. To achieve redress our terms may be severe, they may be stern and even ruthless, but at the same time they can be so just that the country on which they are imposed will feel in its heart that it has no right to complain. But injustice, arrogance, displayed in the hour of triumph, will never be forgotten or forgiven.

For these reasons I am, therefore, strongly averse to transferring more Germans from German rule to the rule of some other nation than can possibly be helped. I cannot conceive any greater cause of future war than that the German people, who have certainly proved themselves one of the most vigorous and powerful races in the world, should be surrounded by a number of small States, many of them consisting of people who have never previously set up a stable government for themselves, but each of them containing large masses of Germans clamouring for reunion with their native land. The proposal of the Polish Commission that we should place 2,100,000 Germans under the control of a people which is of a different religion and which has never proved its capacity for stable self-government throughout its history must, in my judgment, lead sooner or later to a new war in the East of Europe. What I have said about the Germans is equally true of the Magyars. There will never be peace in South-Eastern Europe if every little state now coming into being is to have a large Magyar Irredenta within its borders. I would therefore take as a guiding principle of the peace that as far as is humanly possible the different races should be allocated to their motherlands, and that this human criterion should have precedence over considerations of strategy or economics or communications, which can usually be adjusted by other means. Secondly, I would say that the duration for the payments of reparation ought to disappear if possible with the generation which made the war.

But there is a consideration in favour of a long-sighted peace which influences me even more than the desire to leave no causes justifying a fresh outbreak thirty years hence. There is one element in the present condition of nations which differentiates it from the situation as it was in 1815. In the Napoleonic war the countries were equally exhausted, but the revolutionary spirit had spent its force in the country of its birth, and Germany had satisfied legitimate popular demands for the time being by a series of economic changes which were inspired by courage, foresight and high statesmanship. Even in Russia the Czar had effected great reforms which were probably at that time even too advanced for the half savage population. The situation is very different now. The revolution is still in its infancy. The supreme figures of the Terror are still in command in Russia. The whole of Russia is filled with the spirit of revolution. There is everywhere a deep sense not only of discontent, but of anger and revolt amongst the workmen against pre-war conditions. The whole existing order in its political, social and economic aspects is questioned by the masses of the population from one end of Europe to the other. In some countries, like Germany and Russia, the unrest takes the form of open rebellion; in others, like France, Great Britain and Italy, it takes the shape of strikes and of general disinclination to settle down to work—symptoms which are just as much concerned with the desire for political and social change as with wage demands.

Much of this unrest is healthy. We shall never make a lasting peace by attempting to restore the conditions of 1914. . . .

The greatest danger that I see in the present situation is that Germany may throw in her lot with Bolshevism and place her resources, her brains, her vast organising power at the disposal of the revolutionary fanatics whose dream it is to conquer the world for Bolshevism by force of arms. This danger is no mere chimera. The present Government in Germany is weak; it has no prestige; its authority is challenged; it lingers merely because there is no alternative but the spartacists, and Germany is not ready for spartacism as yet.* . . .

. . . If we are wise, we shall offer to Germany a peace, which, while just, will be preferable for all sensible men to the alternative of Bolshevism. I would, therefore, put it in the forefront of the peace that once she accepts our terms, especially reparation, we will open to her the raw materials and markets of the world on equal terms with ourselves, and will do everything possible to enable the German people to get upon their legs again. We cannot both cripple her and expect her to pay.

Finally, we must offer terms which a responsible Government in Germany can expect to be able to carry out. If we present terms to Germany which are unjust, or excessively onerous, no responsible Government will sign them; . . .

From every point of view, therefore, it seems to me that we ought to endeavour to draw up a peace settlement as if we were impartial arbiters, forgetful of the passions of the war. This settlement ought to have three ends in view. First of all it must do justice to the Allies by taking into account Germany's responsibility for the origin of the war and for the way in which it was fought. Secondly, it must be a settlement which a responsible German Government can sign in the belief that it can fulfil the obligations it incurs. Thirdly, it must be a settlement which will contain in itself no provocations for future wars, and which will constitute an alternative to Bolshevism, because it will commend itself to all reasonable opinion as a fair settlement of the European problem.

II

It is not, however, enough to draw up a just and far-sighted peace with Germany. If we are to offer Europe an alternative to Bolshevism we must make the League of Nations into something which will be both a safeguard to those nations who are prepared for fair dealing with their neighbours, and a menace

* The spartacists were German Communists who were attempting to organize a revolution in Germany after the Imperial government was overthrown.—Ed.

to those who would trespass on the rights of their neighbours, whether they are imperialist empires or imperialist Bolshevists. An essential element, therefore, in the peace settlement is the constitution of the League of Nations as the effective guardian of international right and international liberty throughout the world. If this is to happen the first thing to do is that the leading members of the League of Nations should arrive at an understanding between themselves in regard to armaments. *To my mind it is idle to endeavour to impose a permanent limitation of armaments upon Germany unless we are prepared similarly to impose a limitation upon ourselves.* I recognise that until Germany has settled down and given practical proof that she has abandoned her imperialist ambitions, and until Russia has also given proof that she does not intend to embark upon a military crusade against her neighbours, *it is essential that the leading members of the League of Nations should maintain considerable forces both by land and sea in order to preserve liberty in the world. But if they are to present an united front to the forces both of reaction and revolution, they must arrive at such an agreement in regard to armaments among themselves as would make it impossible for suspicion to arise between the members of the League of Nations in regard to their intentions towards one another. If the League is to do its work for the world it will only be because the members of the League trust it themselves and because there are no apprehensions, rivalries and jealousies in the matter of armaments between them.* The first condition of success for the League of Nations is, therefore, a firm understanding between the British Empire and the United States of America and France and Italy that there will be no competitive building up of fleets or armies between them. Unless this is arrived at before the Covenant is signed the League of Nations will be a sham and a mockery. It will be regarded, and rightly regarded, as a proof that its principal promoters and patrons repose no confidence in its efficacy. But once the leading members of the League have made it clear that they have reached an understanding which will both secure to the League of Nations the strength which is necessary to enable it to protect its members and which at the same time will make misunderstanding and suspicion with regard to competitive armaments impossible between them its future and its authority will be ensured. It will then be able to ensure as an essential condition of peace that not only Germany, but all the smaller States of Europe undertake to limit their armaments and abolish conscription. If the small nations are permitted to organize and maintain conscript armies running each to hundreds of thousands, boundary wars will be inevitable and all Europe will be drawn in. *Unless we secure this universal limitation we shall achieve neither lasting peace, nor the permanent observance of the limitation of German armaments which we now seek to impose.*

I should like to ask why Germany, if she accepts the terms we consider just and fair, should not be admitted to the League of Nations, at any rate as soon as she has established a stable and democratic Government. Would it not be an inducement to her both to sign the terms and to resist Bolshevism? Might it not be safer that she should be inside the League than that she should be outside it?

Finally, I believe that until the authority and effectiveness of the League of Nations has been demonstrated, the British Empire and the United States ought to give to France a guarantee against the possibility of a new German aggression. France has special reason for asking for such a guarantee. She has twice been attacked and twice invaded by Germany in half a century. She has been so attacked because she has been the principal guardian of liberal and democratic civilization against Central European autocracy on the Continent of Europe. It is right that the other great Western democracies should enter into an undertaking which will ensure that they stand by her side in time to protect her against invasion, should Germany ever threaten her again or until the League of Nations has proved its capacity to preserve the peace and liberty of the world.

III

If, however, the Peace Conference is really to secure peace and prove to the world a complete plan of settlement which all reasonable men will recognize as an alternative preferable to anarchy, it must deal with the Russian situation. Bolshevik imperialism does not merely menace the States on Russia's borders. It threatens the whole of Asia and is as near to America as it is to France. It is idle to think that the Peace Conference can separate, however sound a peace it may have arranged with Germany, if it leaves Russia as it is to-day. I do not propose, however, to complicate the question of the peace with Germany by introducing a discussion of the Russian problem. I mention it simply in order to remind ourselves of the importance of dealing with it as soon as possible.

OUTLINE OF PEACE TERMS

Part I

. . . . .

Part II

THE LEAGUE OF NATIONS

(1) All high contracting parties, as part of the Treaty of Peace, to become members of the League of Nations, the Covenant of which will be signed as a separate Treaty by those Powers that are admitted, subject to acceptance of the following conditions:

(i) An agreement between the principal members of the League of Nations in regard to armaments which will put an end to competition between them.

(ii) The lesser members of the League of Nations to accept the limitation of armaments and the abolition of conscription.

(iii) An agreement to be made between all members of the League of Nations for the purpose of securing equal and improved conditions of labour in their respective countries.

Part III

POLITICAL

A. Cession of territory by Germany and the consequential arrangements

EASTERN BOUNDARIES OF GERMANY

(1) Poland to be given a corridor to Danzig, but this to be drawn irrespective of strategic or transportation considerations so as to embrace the smallest possible number of Germans.

(2) Rectification of Bohemian frontier. . . .

WESTERN BOUNDARIES OF GERMANY

(3) No attempt is made to separate the Rhenish Provinces from the rest of Germany. These Provinces to be demilitarised; that is to say, the inhabitants of this territory will not be permitted to bear arms or receive any military training, or to be incorporated in any military organization. . . . As France is naturally anxious about a neighbour who has twice within living memory invaded and devastated her land with surprising rapidity, the British Empire and the United States of America undertake to come to the assistance of France with their whole strength in the event of Germany moving her troops across the Rhine without the consent of the Council of the League of Nations. This guarantee to last until the League of Nations has proved itself to be an adequate security.

(4) Germany to cede Alsace-Lorraine to France.

(5) Germany to cede to France the 1814 frontier, or, in the alternative, in order to compensate France for the destruction of her coal-fields, the present Alsace-Lorraine frontier with the use of the coal-mines in the Saar Valley for a period of 10 years.

Germany to undertake, after the expiration of 10 years, to put no obstacle on the export of the produce of these coal-mines to France.

.   .   .   .   .

NORTHERN BOUNDARIES OF GERMANY

(9) Germany to cede certain portions of Schleswig to Denmark as provided by Danish Commission.

GERMAN OVERSEA POSSESSIONS AND RIGHTS

(10) Germany to cede all rights in the ex-German colonies and in the leased territory of Kiauchow.

.   .   .   .   .

Part IV

REDUCTION OF ARMAMENTS

Preamble explaining that the disarmament of Germany is the first step in the limitation of the armaments of all nations.

(a) Military terms ⎫
(b) Naval terms   ⎬   as already agreed on.
(c) Air terms   ⎭

(d) Questions as to restoration of prisoners of war and interned persons.

(e) Waiver by Germany of all claims on behalf of prisoners of war and interned persons.

Part V

REPARATION

(1) Germany to undertake to pay full reparation to the Allies. It is difficult to assess the amount chargeable against Germany under this head. It certainly greatly exceeds what, on any calculation, Germany is capable of paying. It is therefore suggested that Germany should pay an annual sum for a stated number of years.

This sum to be agreed among the Allied and Associated Powers. Germany to be allowed a number of years within which to work up to payment of the full annual amount.

It has been suggested that a Permanent Commission should be set up to which Germany should be able to appeal for permission to postpone some portion of the annual payment for adequate reasons shown. This Commission would be entitled to cancel the payment of interest on postponed payments during the first few years. The amount received from Germany to be distributed in the following proportions:—

50 per cent. to France;

30 per cent. to the British Empire;

20 per cent. to other nations.

Part of the German payments to be used to liquidate debts owed by the Allies to one another. . . .

10. André Tardieu: Objections to the British Proposals

The French delegation to the Peace Conference was not impressed with the British proposals for a peace treaty. To Clemenceau, Lloyd George's arguments for a more generous policy toward Germany in the matter of territorial boundaries and reparations seemed as dangerous to the position of France as Wilson's Fourteen Points. Consequently he instructed the coordinating leader of his staff of experts, André Tardieu, to prepare a refutation of the British memorandum. Read the text of the French note and try to answer the following questions:

1. What does Tardieu suggest as the more proper way to appease Germany, if such is the desire?
2. What nations other than Germany does France prefer to rely upon as

a barrier against Bolshevism? Why would this kind of policy require
that harsher territorial changes be imposed on Germany?
3. Why does Tardieu think that the British proposals would be unfair to
the other allied nations in Europe?
4. In what sense are the French proposals in the national interest of a
continental land power and the British proposals in the national interest
of a maritime sea power?

I

The French Government is in complete accord with the general
aim of Mr. Lloyd George's Note to make a lasting Peace and for
that a just Peace.

It does not believe on the other hand that this principle, which
is its own, really leads to the conclusions deduced from it in this
Note.

II

This Note suggests granting moderate territorial conditions to
Germany in Europe in order not to leave her after the Peace with
feelings of deep resentment.

This method would be of value if the last war had merely
been for Germany an European war, but this is not the case.

Germany before the war was a great world power whose "future was on the water." It was in this world power that she took
pride. It is this world power that she will not console herself for
having lost.

Now we have taken away from her—or we are going to take
away from her—without being deterred by the fear of her resentment—all her Colonies, all her Navy, a great part of her
merchant Marine (on account of Reparations), her foreign markets in which she was supreme.

Thus we are dealing her the blow which she will feel the worst
and it is hoped to soften it by some improvement in territorial
terms. This is a pure illusion, the remedy is not adequate to the
ill.

If for reasons of general policy, it is desired to give certain satisfactions to Germany, it is not in Europe that they must be sought. This kind of appeasement will be vain so long as Germany is cut off from world politics.

In order to appease Germany (if such is the desire) we must offer her colonial satisfactions, naval satisfactions, satisfactions of commercial expansion. But the Note of March 26 merely contemplates giving her European territorial satisfactions.

III

Mr. Lloyd George's Note fears that if the territorial conditions imposed on Germany are too severe, it will give an impetus to Bolshevism. Is it not to be feared that this would be precisely the result of the action suggested?

The Conference has decided to call to life a certain number of new States. Can it without committing an injustice sacrifice them out of regard for Germany by imposing upon them inacceptable frontiers? If these peoples—notably Poland and Bohemia—have so far resisted Bolshevism, they have done so by the development of national spirit. If we do violence to this sentiment, they will become the prey of Bolshevism and the only barrier now existing between Russian Bolshevism and German Bolshevism will be broken down.

The result will be either a Confederation of Central and Eastern Europe under the leadership of Bolshevist Germany or the enslavement of this same vast territory by Germany swung back to reaction after a period of general anarchy. In either case, the Allies will have lost the war.

The policy of the French Government is on the contrary to give strong support to these young nations with the help of all that is liberal in Europe and not to seek at their expense to attenuate—which besides would be useless—the colonial, naval and commercial disaster which the Peace inflicts on Germany.

If in order to give to these young nations frontiers which are essential to their national life, it is necessary to transfer to their sovereignty Germans, the sons of those who enslaved them, one may regret having to do this and do it only with measure, but it cannot be avoided.

Moreover, by depriving Germany totally and definitely of her colonies because she has ill-treated the natives, one forfeits the right to refuse to Poland or to Bohemia their natural frontiers on the ground that Germans have occupied their territory as the forerunners of Pan-Germanism.

IV

The Note of March 26 insists—and the French Government is in complete agreement—on the necessity of making a Peace that will appear to Germany to be a just Peace.

But it may be remarked that taking German mentality into consideration, it is not sure that the Germans will have the same idea of what is just as the Allies have.

Finally it must be retained that this impression of justice must be felt not only by the enemy but also, and first of all, by the Allies. The Allies who have fought together must conclude a Peace which will be fair to all of them.

But what would be the result of following the method suggested in the Note of March 26?

A certain number of full and final guarantees would be ensured to the maritime nations which have never been invaded.

Full and final cession of the German colonies.

Full and final surrender of the German Navy.

Full and final surrender of a large part of the German merchant Marine.

Full and lasting, if not final, exclusion of Germany from foreign markets.

To the continental nations, however, that is to say to those who have suffered the most from the war, only partial and deferred solutions are offered.

Partial solutions such as the reduced frontier suggested for Poland and Bohemia.

Deferred solutions such as the defensive undertaking offered to France for the protection of her territory.

Deferred solutions such as the proposed arrangement for the Sarre coal.

There is here an inequality which may well have a disastrous influence on the after-war relations between the Allies, which are more important than the after-war relations between Germany and the Allies.

It has been shown in Paragraph I that it would be an illusion to hope to find in territorial satisfactions given to Germany a sufficient compensation for the world-wide disaster she has sustained. May it be permitted to add that it would be an injustice to make the weight of these compensations fall upon those of the Allied nations which have borne the brunt of the war.

These countries cannot bear the costs of the Peace after having borne the cost of the war. It is essential that they too shall have the feeling that the Peace is just and equal for all.

Failing this, it is not only Central Europe in which Bolshevism may be feared, for as events have shown, no atmosphere is more favourable to Bolshevism than that of national disappointment.

V

The French Government desires to confine itself for the time being to these considerations of general policy.

It pays full homage to the intentions which inspire Mr. Lloyd George's Note, but it believes that the considerations which the present Note deduces from it are in accord with justice and the general interest.

It is by these considerations that the French Government will be guided in the coming exchange of views during the discussion of the terms suggested by the Prime Minister of Great Britain.

In our final group of readings, we shall examine some appraisals of Wilsonian diplomacy that have been made by historians and political scientists. All four writers in this section of the readings have used some of the same documents that are included in this volume and many more besides.

The interpretations by these historians and political scientists are written with the assumption that the reader already knows something about the results of the Peace Conference at Paris. Hence, as you read these selections, it would be well for you to keep in mind the major provisions of the peace treaties that were prepared in 1919–1921. To help you do this, a full-scale summary of the work of the Paris Conference has been included as the opening selection.

Wilson's Peace Program as Viewed by Recent Historians and Political Scientists

11. THE PEACE SETTLEMENT: A SUMMARY

Paris was chosen for the site of the peace conference. The French insisted on it, and it seemed to the other Allied nations to deserve that honor since France had borne the heaviest burden of the war. Yet the choice of the French capital meant that the peace settlement would inevitably have a symbolic imprint of triumph and revenge, especially for the German people.

Wilson, however, was so determined to fight for a peace based upon his principles that he decided to attend the conference in person. This was absolutely unprecedented in American history; no president had ever left the country before, and never since Wilson's time has any American president been away for so long a time.

As a result, the Paris Peace Conference became a kind of summit conference attended by the heads of the Allied governments as well as foreign ministers and diplomatic advisors. In addition to about seventy heads of government and foreign ministers, there were over a thousand experts and advisors, plus an equal number of clerks and typists. Furthermore, Paris became the center for all kinds of ethnic groups who demanded a hearing for their grievances and aspirations. There were Irish, Finns, Estonians, Letts, Lithuanians, Ukranians, Ruthenians, Albanians, Egyptians, Zionists, Lebanese, Syrians, Koreans, Indians, Malaysians, to mention only a few. From the start it was apparent that peacemaking would take place in the midst of a tremendous amount of cross-pressures affecting a great number and variety of national and selfish interests. Furthermore, the leaders of the Allied governments were apprehensive about the conspicuous absence of Russia and the threat of Bolshevism.

It was impossible, therefore, to maintain Wilson's principle of "open covenants openly arrived at" in any literal way. The Peace Conference opened with a plenary session of all the delegates on January 18, 1919; but this was largely a formality. It was quickly decided to center all discussion in the hands of a Council of Ten representing the five Great Powers, to exclude press representatives, and to issue brief communiques about their deliberations. Of course all decisions were to be submitted for ratification to the plenary sessions of the Conference, but the real work was done in the specialized committees which gathered a vast array of historical data and statistics for the leaders in the Council of Ten.

The Council of Ten was composed of the leaders of the four great Allied powers—the United States, Great Britain, France, and Italy—plus the two leaders of the Japanese delegation. Later, the Japanese and the foreign ministers tended to drop out, and the key decisions were made by the inner circle of the "Big Four": Woodrow Wilson and the three prime ministers of England, France, and Italy—David Lloyd George, Georges Clemenceau, and Vittorio Orlando. When the Italian delegation left the Conference over the Fiume dispute, the remaining "Big Three" dominated the deliberations of the Conference.

Despite the enormous problems that had to be faced in regard to territorial settlements—the drafting of the League Covenant, the military occupation of the Rhineland, the payment of reparations by Germany, and the disposition of the former German colonies—much of the major work of the Peace Conference was completed within six months after its official opening, although final treaties in the Balkans and Asia Minor took several months longer to complete. The settlement that emerged from the Peace Conference is called the Peace of Paris, and the individual treaties that constituted the Peace of Paris bear the names of the small towns near Paris where they were signed.

Overshadowing all others in importance was the Treaty of Versailles with Germany. It was signed with great ceremony in the Hall of Mirrors in the palace of Versailles where the German representatives were handed the treaty on a take-it-or-else basis. The terms of the treaty were harsh but, because of Wilson's resistance, they were not nearly as harsh as the French wished them to be. Both in the east and the west, the German frontiers were contracted. In the west, Alsace-Lorraine was returned to France, and the French also received the right to exploit the rich industrial resources of the Saar basin adjacent to Luxembourg. Two small strips of land were awarded to Belgium and Denmark. In the east, a corridor of land giving the reconstituted nation of Poland access to the sea separated East Prussia from the west of Germany. The German-speaking seaport of Danzig near the mouth of the Vistula River, however, was set up as a Free City under the supervision of the League of Nations. In addition, all former German colonies in the western Pacific Ocean and in Africa were transferred to Japan, England, and other countries in the British Commonwealth under the "mandate system" of the League of Nations.

The military terms of the treaty were equally severe. Germany was forbidden to build offensive weapons such as airplanes and submarines, and the size of the German army was limited to a small professional force of 100,000 men. The German navy was also limited to a puny size. In addition, the Allies provided for a fifteen-year military occupation of the left bank of the Rhine and imposed a demilitarized zone thirty miles wide on the right bank.

The reparations clauses of the treaty placed a heavy and indeterminate burden of payments on Germany. Pending the working out of details, the Germans were required to turn over $5 billions in reparations payments within two years, after which they would be presented with a final total. Everyone expected it to be huge and to require several decades to pay off. And to justify such demands, there was Article 231 of the treaty which required Germans to acknowledge their primary guilt in causing the bloody and destructive world war.

The settlements with Germany's allies followed the same general pattern. The Treaty of St. Germain with Austria (September 10, 1919) left the once-proud Austrians bereft of their central European empire. They saw three million German-speaking compatriots assigned to the new state of Czechoslovakia, and a quarter of a million Austrians were assigned to Italy in the new territorial adjustments that embraced the former Austrian port of Trieste and the South Tyrol.

The Treaty of Trianon with Hungary (June 4, 1920) reduced the historic kingdom of Hungary far beyond any reasonable claims based on ethnic considerations. Almost two-thirds of its Magyar speaking inhabitants were assigned to Czechoslovakia, Rumania, and Yugoslavia.

The Treaty of Neuilly with Bulgaria (November 27, 1919) was comparatively mild. Small areas of land were assigned to Greece, Rumania, and Yugoslavia in the rearrangement of the frontiers by the Peace Conference. The final treaty—the Treaty of Sèvres with Turkey (August, 1920)—ratified the liberation of the Arab states in the Middle East, although the more important of them were placed under the temporary supervision of France and England subject to the mandate provisions of the League.

A fundamental part of the Peace of Paris, of course, was the creation of the League of Nations. In fact, the Covenant of the League comprised the first twenty-six articles of the various peace treaties which were signed at Paris. The original or "charter" members of the League were the signatory states who ratified the Treaty. In addition any other self-governing state could be admitted to the League of Nations by a two-thirds vote of the Assembly, provided that it gave effective guarantees of its sincere intention to observe its international obligations and to accept such regulations as might be prescribed by the League concerning its military and naval forces. Any member of the League could withdraw after two years' notice of its intention to do so.

The League of Nations was to function through the instrumentality of an assembly, a council, and a permanent secretariat. The Assembly constituted the main representative body of the League where each member state had one vote and not more than three representatives. According to the Covenant, the Assembly was empowered to deal with "any matter within the sphere of action of the League or affecting the peace of the world." In practice, the Assembly controlled the budget of the League, elected non-permanent members of the Council, admitted new states to membership, and participated in the election of judges to a Permanent Court of International Justice set up as part of the international machinery to deal with disputes among nations.

The Council was to be composed of five permanent and four non-permanent members, but the refusal of the United States to enter the League left only four permanent members. When Germany was admitted to the League in 1926, the number of permanent members was fixed at five, and the number of non-permanent members was fixed at nine. A permanent seat was also given to Soviet Russia in 1934 when that country was admitted to the League.

The permanent secretariat was an important adjunct to the Council and Assembly. It comprised a Secretary-General and a large staff which he administered with the aid of two deputy secretaries-general. In general, the Secretariat was to carry on the essential bureaucratic duties of the League.

Presumably the chief purpose of those who formulated the League of Nations was to prevent future wars. To this end, Article 10 bound the member states "to respect and preserve against external aggression the territorial integrity and existing independence of all Members of the League"; and Article 11 declared that it was "the friendly right of each member of the League to bring to the attention of the Assembly or of the Council any circumstance whatever affecting international relations which threatens to disturb international peace or the good understanding between nations upon which peace depends."

Other articles encouraged the use of arbitration and mediation by member states who found themselves involved in disputes and required them to submit to the Council any dispute likely to lead to a rupture which could not be settled by arbitration. In case of mediation by the Council, parties to the dispute were to be asked to submit relevant facts and papers which would enable the Council to examine the dispute and make recommendations. In most cases the decision of the Council had to be unanimous, and all members were expected to support such a decision.

Any member of the League who went to war in disregard of its agreements to resort to arbitration, mediation, or judicial settlement would be subject to drastic penalties; Article 16 provided that all other members should agree "immediately to subject it to the severance of all trade or financial relations" (economic sanctions). In addition the Council might also "recommend to the several governments concerned what effective military, naval, or air forces the Members of the League shall severally contribute to the armed forces to be used to protect the covenants of the League."

Great care was taken to stipulate that the Council should have no right to intervene in any matter which by international law was solely within the domestic jurisdiction of any one of the States. On the other hand, the Council had administrative and supervisory tasks in relation to the Saar Basin, the Free City of Danzig, and the mandatory system created by the Peace of Paris.

The former German colonies and the Arab land once under Turkish rule were assigned to three classes of mandated territories. Class A mandates included such former Turkish possessions as Iraq, Syria, Lebanon, Palestine, and Transjordan which were considered to have reached a stage of development in which their independence could be provisionally recognized and full independence achieved quickly with the help of technical and administrative assistance. Class B mandates included the former German colonies in Central Africa where a longer period of tutelage would be required. Class C mandates included such former German colonies as Southwest Africa and her Pacific Islands where their "remoteness from the center of civilization" and other circumstances made it desirable to place them under the laws of another nation subject to safeguards for the native populations. These Class C mandates quickly became a thinly veiled form of annexation carried out by Japan and the Union of South Africa. Nevertheless, the Permanent Mandates Commission of the League did attempt to keep the mandated territories under a close watch. To that extent, therefore, the old ways of European colonialism were being brought under the scrutiny of world public opinion.

In the last analysis, the Peace of Paris, in spite of its imper-

fections and its severity towards the defeated powers, created
boundaries for the European state system that came closer to
coinciding with ethnic groupings than any previous peace settlement; and, what is more, it created the machinery for a new international order and for the future revision of the peace terms
through the League of Nations.

12. Richard Hofstadter: Wilson's Peace Program

*Richard Hofstadter of Columbia University is well known for his
many writings concerning the political and intellectual history of
the United States. In one of his works Professor Hofstadter has
developed provocative portraits of such progressive leaders as
Theodore Roosevelt and Woodrow Wilson. The following selection is taken from the chapter on Woodrow Wilson which was
written for THE AMERICAN POLITICAL TRADITION (1948).
As you read it, keep the following questions in mind:*

1. According to Hofstadter, what were the most serious limitations in
   Wilson's conception of international economic relations?
2. Why does Hofstadter maintain that Wilson's struggle with Clemenceau
   and Lloyd George was "not a struggle between an Old Order and a New
   Order, but merely a quarrel as to how the Old Order should settle its
   affairs"?

. . . The program Wilson took to Paris envisioned a world
order based upon national self-determination, free trade, and
a League of Nations to keep the peace. "What we seek," he explained, "is the reign of law, based upon the consent of the governed and sustained by the organized opinion of mankind." National self-determination, the international equivalent of democ-

racy in domestic politics, would embody the principle of consent of the governed. Free trade would soften national rivalries and broaden prosperity. The League was to give security to the whole system through mutual guarantees of territorial integrity and common action against an aggressor.

Conspicuously absent from the Fourteen Points was any meaningful demand for a substantial change in international economic relations. Eight of the Fourteen Points applied the doctrine of self-determination to specific parts of Europe. The remaining six points were of general application, and of these only three dealt with economic matters: freedom of the seas in peace and in war, the removal of all economic barriers between nations, and an impartial adjustment of colonial claims. Not one of these three points represented anything more than a pious hope, and not one was even remotely realized in fact. The structure of colonial claims was hardly touched by the mandate system of the League. Freedom of the seas had to be waived at the outset upon the insistence of the British, who would not even indulge in the hypocrisy of endorsing it on principle. The removal of economic barriers was an idle suggestion if one could not remove the economic and social structures, the profit motives and systems of domestic business power that made trade barriers inevitable. Wilson dared not even try to commit his own country to further removal of trade barriers—and it was the United States that actually began international tariff warfare in the postwar era. Finally, the idea of multiplying national sovereignties and expecting a reduction of international trade barriers to follow was certainly tempting the wrath of the gods.

The peace that was signed at Versailles was a political peace in which the fundamental economic arrangements of nineteenth-century Europe were taken for granted. Wilson himself told his commission of American experts that he was "not much interested in the economic subjects" that might be discussed at Paris; and John Maynard Keynes has remarked that "the fundamental economic problems of a Europe starving and disintegrating before their eyes was the one question in which it was impossible to arouse the interest of the Four." Thorstein Veblen wrote in 1919 that the Covenant of the League

is a political document, an instrument of realpolitik, created in the image of nineteenth century imperialism. It has been set up by political statesmen, on political grounds, for political ends, and with political apparatus to be used with political effects. . . . True to the political tradition, the Covenant provides for enforcing the peace by recourse to arms and commercial hostilities, but it contemplates no measures for avoiding war by avoiding the status quo out of which the great war arose.

Wilson, in short, failed again to grapple with economics, as he had failed to grapple with it in the political theory of his academic years. During his career in practical politics he had learned to mold his appeal along the lines of group and class interests and to resolve political conflicts into economic issues, but somehow when he stepped into the world theater he lapsed once again into the intellectual primness and gentility of the old-fashioned professor who had been enthralled with what he thought was the disinterestedness of the great British statesmen, and who had said of the American Senate in the Gilded Age that it was "divorced from class interests." The end of his career was full of contradictions, in which the Wilson of *Congressional Government** struggled with the Wilson who had acquired a more mature and realistic education in American party battles. What he said about the causes of the war had little relation to the manner in which he made the peace.

In an address on September 27, 1918 he had declared:

Special alliances and economic rivalries and hostilities have been the prolific source in the modern world of the plans and passions that produce war. It would be an insincere as

* Hofstadter is referring to a book written by Wilson when he was beginning his career as a professor of political science.—Ed.

well as insecure peace that did not exclude them in definite
and binding terms.

Having made just such an insecure peace, he returned to the
United States to defend it, and in the course of his defense said
again at St. Louis, September 5, 1919:

> Why, my fellow citizens, is there any man here or any
> woman, let me say is there any child here, who does not know
> that the seed of war in the modern world is industrial and
> commercial rivalry? The real reason that the war that we
> have just finished took place was that Germany was afraid
> her commercial rivals were going to get the better of her, and
> the reason why some nations went into the war against Ger-
> many was that they thought Germany would get the com-
> mercial advantage of them. . . . This war, in its inception
> was a commercial and industrial war. It was not a political
> war.

No wonder, then, that Wilson's League, which was not intended or designed to change the system of commercial and industrial rivalries, was inadequate to prevent war. Europe, desperately in need of economic unity under large-scale industrial tech-
nology, was partitioned into an increased number of economically
unstable and strategically indefensible small states. Germany, the
economic hub of the Continent, was crippled in so far as Britain
and France found it in their power to do. This disorganized and
broken world of competing nationalist enterprises the League
was expected to preserve and make secure. The League itself
did not represent a vital change, but simply an attempt to give
organization to the old chaos.

No matter how historians may dramatize Wilson's struggle with
Clemenceau and Lloyd George, it was not a struggle between
an Old Order and a New Order, but merely a quarrel as to how
the Old Order should settle its affairs. In this attempt to organize
and regulate a failing system of competitive forces the theme of

Wilson's domestic leadership was repeated on a world scale. Just as the New Freedom* had been, under the idealistic form of a crusade for the rights and opportunities of the small man, an effort to restore the archaic conditions of nineteenth-century competition, so the treaty and the League Covenant were an attempt, in the language of democracy, peace, and self-determination, to retain the competitive national state system of the nineteenth century without removing the admitted source of its rivalries and animosities. It had always been Wilson's aim to preserve the essentials of the *status quo* by reforming it; but failing essentially to reform, he was unable in the end to preserve.

In March 1919 Wilson's old friend of the New Jersey period, George L. Record, who had played a large part in converting him to progressivism, sent him a remarkable letter, analyzing the inadequacy of Wilson's conceptions to the present era. Wilson, Record wrote frankly, had

> ignored the great issue which is slowly coming to the front, the question of economic democracy, abolition of privilege, and securing to men the full fruits of their labor or service.
>
> There is no glory . . . in standing for the principles of political democracy . . . [which] is like standing for the Ten Commandments. . . .
>
> The issue of political democracy has passed. The issue is now one of industrial or economic democracy.
>
> The League of Nations idea will not help your position, either now or in history, because, like all your other policies, it does not go to the root of the problem. Wars are caused by privilege. Every modern state is governed by the privileged, that is, by those who control industry by owning railroads, lands, mines, banks, and credit. These men thus obtain enormous and unearned capital, for which there is no use in the country where it is produced, because the poverty of the

---

* The "New Freedom" was the phrase that Wilson used to identify his principles and program when he came to the Presidency.—Ed.

workers limits the home market. Those who control this sur-
plus capital must seek new countries and new people to exploit, and this clash of selfish interests leads to war. The cure
for war is the reign of justice, i.e., the abolition of privilege
in each of the great nations. I do not believe that you can
set up machinery which will maintain justice in international
relations among governments which deny justice to their own
people. If the League works, it will be when and to the extent that justice is established within the countries which are
parties to the League. Indeed, it is entirely possible, if not
probable, that such a league established by the present governments of the Allies, if it has any real power, is very likely
to be used as an international bulwark of privilege. That
danger looms large after you pass off the scene. . . .

Record urged Wilson to supplement his international program
with a social-democratic program at home, including a demand
for public-utility ownership and limitation of great fortunes. It
might be impossible to realize this program, he admitted, but
Wilson's failure would be only temporary. Future generations
would recognize his wisdom and acclaim him "a truly great
man."

Wilson acknowledged Record's letter cordially. Almost a year
before receiving it he had expressed somewhat similar sentiments
to Professor Axson. The two were talking about the qualifications
of the next president, and Wilson remarked that he must be a
philosophical man, capable of thinking in world terms. At present,
"the only really internationally minded people are the labor
people."

The world is going to change radically, and I am satisfied
that governments will have to do many things which are now
left to individuals and corporations. I am satisfied for instance that the government will have to take over all the
great natural resources . . . all the water power, all the coal

mines, all the oil fields, etc. They will have to be government-owned.

If I should say that outside, people would call me a socialist, but I am not a socialist. And it is because I am not a socialist that I believe these things. I think the only way we can prevent communism is by some such action as that. . . .

But if Wilson's private convictions were really evolving from American progressivism to an international social-democratic point of view, the fact is not registered in his public policies. The last part of his career seems like the work of a somnambulist who repeats unerringly his appointed workday rounds while his mind moves in an insulated shadow world. If he believed his fine statements with the depth and emphasis with which he made them, he may well have accounted his career as a world statesman a series of failures. He appealed for neutrality in thought and deed, and launched upon a diplomatic policy that is classic for its partisanship. He said that American entrance into the war would be a world calamity, and led the nation in. He said that only a peace between equals would last, and participated in the *Diktat* of Versailles. He said that the future security of the world depended on removing the economic causes of war, and did not attempt even to discuss these causes at the Peace Conference. He declared his belief in the future of government ownership, and allowed his administration to close in a riot of reaction. He wanted desperately to bring the United States into the League, and launched on a course of action that made American participation impossible. No wonder that in one of his moments of apprehension he should have confessed to George Creel: "What I seem to see—with all my heart I hope that I am wrong—is a tragedy of disappointment."

And yet it is his hopes and promises that make Wilson's record seem so bleak. Set against the dark realities, it is defensible. In the Fourteen Points he produced a more sane and liberal, if not enduring, basis for peace than anyone else among the belligerents. By appealing to the hopes of Germany he helped to bring an earlier armistice. Harsh as the treaty was, it would have been materially worse without his influence. He went to Europe handicapped by his apparent repudiation in the Congressional elections of 1918, limited by the national claims and secret treaties of his allies, tied to the technique of compromise by his hopes for the League, committed by his belief in capitalism and nationalism to accept the major consequences of the disaster they had wrought. Confronted time and time again at Paris with a series of insoluble dilemmas, faced with too many battles on too many fronts, he became, in Charles Seymour's words, "the plaything of events." Granting the severe limitations imposed upon his work by the logic of the situation, Paul Birdsall, in his *Versailles Twenty Years After,* finds "an extraordinary consistency in Wilson's fight for his program under overwhelming difficulties, as well as a high degree of political intelligence in translating the abstract principles of his program into concrete details of application."

Clemenceau habitually dozed off when matters unrelated to French security were under consideration at the Conference. Lloyd George on more than one occasion admitted lightheartedly his ignorance of some of the most elementary facts of European economics and geography. ("Please refresh my memory," he once asked an aide. "Is it Upper or Lower Silesia that we are giving away?") Wilson begged his experts: "Tell me what is right and I will fight for it. Give me a guaranteed position," and went down on hands and knees in his suite until the small hours of the mornings, poring over maps and charts, trying to master the complicated maze of fact involved in the negotiations. Although he felt obliged to defend the peace in the United States, sometimes in incredible language—"a people's treaty," "the great humane document of all time"—he well knew how vulnerable it was. His remark that the much-criticized Shantung settlement was the best that could be salvaged from "a dirty past" might well have been his verdict on the treaty as a whole.

One thing, he believed, might save the whole structure—the Covenant of the League. The effort to save the League became a matter of the most desperate psychological urgency for him. His plans had been hamstrung, his hopes abandoned one after another, until nothing but the League was left. The New Freedom, as he had predicted, had disappeared in the war, and a liberal democratic peace had gone by the board at Paris. The League was now a question of moral salvation or annihilation, for everything he stood for hung in the balance. If a lasting peace were not realized, what justification could he find for having led his country into war? His sense of guilt hung over him like a cloud. In the American cemetery at Suresnes he broke out fervently: "I sent these lads over here to die. Shall I—can I—ever speak a word of counsel which is inconsistent with the assurances I gave them when I came over?" In the long speech delivered at Pueblo on the day he suffered his stroke, he made a striking confession:

Again and again . . . mothers who lost their sons in France have come to me and, taking my hand, have shed tears upon it not only, but they have added, "God bless you, Mr. President!" Why . . . should they pray God to bless me? I advised the Congress of the United States to create the situation that led to the death of their sons. I ordered their sons oversea. I consented to their sons being put in the most difficult parts of the battle line, where death was certain, as in the impenetrable difficulties of the forest of Argonne. Why should they weep upon my hand and call down the blessings of God upon me? Because they believe that their boys died for something that vastly transcends any of the immediate and palpable objects of the war. They believe, and rightly believe, that their sons saved the liberty of the world.

13. Hans Morgenthau: The National Interest vs. Moral Abstractions

Hans Morgenthau is one of the leading advocates of a hard-headed realism in foreign policy. In addition to his own writings, his efforts as director of the Center for the Study of American Foreign Policy at the University of Chicago have encouraged other important contributions to the study of the principles and problems of international politics. The following selection is taken from an article which attracted widespread notice when it appeared in the American Political Science Review. *Consider the following questions as you read it:*

1. According to Morgenthau, what three types of statesmen have shaped the development of American foreign policy?
2. Which conception of foreign policy does Wilson represent, and how do his principles differ from those followed in earlier periods of our history?
3. Why does Morgenthau think that Wilson's efforts resulted in "a triple failure"?

. . . The illusion that a nation can escape, if it only wants to, from power politics into a realm where action is guided by moral principles rather than by considerations of power, not only is deeply rooted in the American mind; it also took more than a century for this illusion to crowd out the older notion that international politics is an unending struggle for power in which the interests of individual nations must necessarily be defined in terms of power. Out of the struggle between these two opposing conceptions three types of American statesmen emerge: the realist, thinking in terms of power and represented by Alexander Hamilton; the ideological, acting in terms of power, thinking in terms of moral principles, and represented by Thomas Jefferson and John Quincy Adams; the moralist, thinking and acting in terms of moral principles and represented by Woodrow Wilson.

From Hans Morgenthau, "The Mainsprings of American Foreign Policy: National Interest vs. Moral Abstractions," *The American Political Science Review,* 44 (Dec. 1950), 840–849. Reprinted with permission.

To these three types, three periods of American foreign policy roughly correspond: the first covering the first decade of the history of the United States as an independent nation, the second covering the nineteenth century to the Spanish-American War, the third covering the half century after that war. That this division of the history of American foreign policy refers only to prevailing tendencies and does by no means preclude the operation side by side of different tendencies in the same period, will become obvious in the discussion.

It illustrates both the depth of the moralist illusion and the original strength of the opposition to it that the issue between these two opposing conceptions of foreign policy was joined at the very beginning of the history of the United States, decided in favor of the realist position, and formulated with unsurpassed simplicity and penetration by Alexander Hamilton. The memorable occasion was Washington's proclamation of neutrality in the War of the First Coalition against revolutionary France.

In 1792, the War of the First Coalition had ranged Austria, Prussia, Sardinia, Great Britain, and the United Netherlands against revolutionary France, which was tied to the United States by a treaty of alliance. On April 22, 1793, Washington issued a proclamation of neutrality, and it was in defense of that proclamation that Hamilton wrote the "Pacificus" and "Americanus" articles. Among the arguments directed against the proclamation were three derived from moral principles. Faithfulness to treaty obligations, gratitude toward a country which had lent its assistance to the colonies in their struggle for independence, and the affinity of republican institutions were cited to prove that the United States must side with France. Against these moral principles, Hamilton invoked the national interest of the United States:

There would be no proportion between the mischiefs and perils to which the United States would expose themselves, by embarking in the war, and the benefit which the nature of their stipulation aims at securing to France, or that which it would be in their power actually to render her by becoming a party.

This disproportion would be a valid reason for not executing the guaranty. All contracts are to receive a reasonable construction. Self-preservation is the first duty of a nation; and though in the performance of stipulations relating to war, good faith requires that its ordinary hazards should be fairly met, because they are directly contemplated by such stipulations, yet it does not require that extraordinary and extreme hazards should be run. . . .

The basis of gratitude is a benefit received or intended, which there was no right to claim, originating in a regard to the interest or advantage of the party on whom the benefit is, or is meant to be, conferred. If a service is rendered from views relative to the immediate interest of the party who performs it, and is productive of reciprocal advantages, there seems scarcely, in such a case, to be an adequate basis for sentiment like that of gratitude. . . . It may be affirmed as a general principle, that the predominant motive of good offices from one nation to another, is the interest or advantage of the nation which performs them.

Indeed, the rule of morality in this respect is not precisely the same between nations as between individuals. The duty of making its own welfare the guide of its actions, is much stronger upon the former than upon the latter; in proportion to the greater magnitude and importance of national compared with individual happiness, and to the greater permanency of the effects of national than of individual conduct. Existing millions, and for the most part future generations, are concerned in the present measures of a government; while the consequences of the private actions of an individual ordinarily terminate with himself, or are circumscribed within a narrow compass.

Whence it follows that an individual may, on numerous

occasions, meritoriously indulge the emotions of generosity and benevolence, not only without an eye to, but even at the expense of, his own interest. But a government can rarely, if at all, be justifiable in pursuing a similar course; and, if it does so, ought to confine itself within much stricter bounds. . . .

Must a nation subordinate its security, its happiness, nay, its very existence to the respect for treaty obligations, to the sentiment of gratitude, to sympathy with a kindred political system? This was the question which Hamilton proposed to answer, and his answer was an unequivocal "no." Hamilton unswervingly applied one standard to the issues raised by the opposition to Washington's proclamation of neutrality: the national interest of the United States. He put the legalistic and moralistic arguments of the opposition, represented by Madison under the pseudonym "Helvidius," into the context of the concrete power situation in which the United States found itself on the international scene and asked: If the United States were to join France against virtually all of Europe, what risks would the United States run, what advantages could it expect, what good could it do for its ally?

Considerations such as these, recognized for what they are, have guided American foreign policy but for a short period, that is, as long as the Federalists were in power. *The Federalist* and Washington's Farewell Address are their classic expression. Yet these considerations, not recognized for what they are, sometimes even rejected, have determined the great objectives of American foreign policy to this day. During the century following their brief flowering, they have by and large continued to influence policies as well, under the cover, as it were, of those moral principles with which from Jefferson onward American statesmen have liked to justify their moves on the international scene. Thus this second period witnessed a discrepancy between political thought and political action, yet a coincidence in the intended results of both. What was said of Gladstone could also have been said of Jefferson, John Quincy Adams, Theodore Roosevelt, the war policies of Wilson and Franklin D. Roosevelt: what the moral law demanded was by a felicitous coincidence always identical with what the national interest seemed to require. Political thought and political action moved on different planes, which, however, were so inclined as to merge in the end.

John Quincy Adams is the classic example of the political moralist in thought and word who cannot help being a political realist in action. Yet even in Jefferson, whose dedication to abstract morality was much stronger and whose realist touch in foreign affairs was much less sure, the moral pretense yielded often, especially in private utterance, to the impact of the national interest upon native good sense.

Thus during the concluding decade of the Napoleonic Wars Jefferson's thought on international affairs was a reflection of the ever-changing distribution of power in the world rather than of immutable moral principles. In 1806, he favored "an English ascendancy on the ocean" as being "safer for us than that of France." In 1807, he was by the logic of events forced to admit:

> I never expected to be under the necessity of wishing success to Buonaparte. But the English being equally tyrannical at sea as he is on land, & that tyranny bearing on us in every point of either honor or interest, I say, "down with England" and as for what Buonaparte is then to do to us, let us trust to the chapter of accidents, I cannot, with the Anglomen, prefer a certain present evil to a future hypothetical one.

However, in 1812, when Napoleon was at the pinnacle of his power, Jefferson hoped for the restoration of the balance of power. Speaking of England, he said that

> it is for the general interest that she should be a sensible and independent weight in the scale of nations, and be able to contribute, when a favorable moment presents itself, to re-

duce under the same order, her great rival in flagitiousness. We especially ought to pray that the powers of Europe may be so poised and counterpoised among themselves, that their own security may require the presence of all their forces at home, leaving the other quarters of the globe in undisturbed tranquility.

In 1814, again compelled by the logic of events, he came clearly out against Napoleon and in favor of a balance of power which would leave the power of Napoleon and of England limited, but intact:

Surely none of us wish to see Bonaparte conquer Russia, and lay thus at his feet the whole continent of Europe. This done, England would be but a breakfast; and, although I am free from the visionary fears which the votaries of England have effected to entertain, because I believe he cannot effect the conquest of Europe; yet put all Europe into his hands, and he might spare such a force to be sent in British ships, as I would as leave not have to encounter, when I see how much trouble a handful of British soldiers in Canada has given us. No. It cannot be to our interest that all Europe should be reduced to a single monarchy. The true line of interest for us, is, that Bonaparte should be able to effect the complete exclusion of England from the whole continent of Europe, in order, as the same letter said, "by this peaceable engine of constraint, to make her renounce her views of dominion over the ocean, of permitting no other nation to navigate it but with her license, and on tribute to her, and her aggressions on the persons of our citizens who may choose to exercise their right of passing over that element." And this would be effected by Bonaparte's succeeding so far as to close the Baltic against her. This success I wished him the last year, this I wish him this year; but were he again advanced to Moscow, I should again wish him such disasters as would prevent his reaching Petersburg. And were the consequences even to be the longer continuance of our war, I would rather meet them than see the whole force of Europe wielded by a single hand.

Similarly, in 1815, Jefferson wrote:

For my part, I wish that all nations may recover and retain their independence; that those which are overgrown may not advance beyond safe measures of power, that a salutary balance may be ever maintained among nations, and that our peace, commerce, and friendship, may be sought and cultivated by all.

It was only when, after 1815, the danger to the balance of power seemed to have passed that Jefferson allowed himself again to indulge in the cultivation of moral principles divorced from the political exigencies of the hour.

From this tendency to which Jefferson only too readily yielded, John Quincy Adams was well-nigh immune. We are here in the presence of a statesman who had been reared in the realist tradition of the first period of American foreign policy, who had done the better part of his work of statecraft in an atmosphere saturated with Jeffersonian principles, and who had achieved the merger of these two elements of his experience into an harmonious whole. Between John Quincy Adams' moral principles and the traditional interest of the United States there was hardly ever a conflict. The moral principles were nothing but the political interests formulated in moral terms, and vice versa. They fit the interests as a glove fits the hand. Adams' great contributions to the tradition of American foreign policy, freedom of the seas, the Monroe Doctrine, and Manifest Destiny, are witness to this achievement.

The legal and moral principle of the freedom of the seas was in the hands of Adams a weapon, as it had been two centuries earlier in the hands of Grotius wielded on behalf of the Low Countries, through which an inferior naval power endeavored to safeguard its independence against Great Britain, the mistress of the seas. The Monroe Doctrine's moral postulates of anti-imperialism and mutual non-intervention were the negative conditions for the safety and enduring greatness of the United States. Their fulfillment vouchsafed the isolation of the United States from the power struggles of Europe and, through it, the continuing predominance of the United States in the Western Hemisphere. Manifest Destiny was the moral justification as well as the moral incentive for the westward expansion of the United States, the peculiar American way—foreordained by the objective conditions of American existence—of founding an empire, the "American Empire," as one of the contemporary opponents of Adams' policies put it.

Jefferson and John Quincy Adams stand at the beginning of the second period of American thought on foreign policy, both its most eminent representatives and the heirs of a realist tradition which continued to mould political action, while it had largely ceased to influence political thought. At the beginning of the third period, McKinley leads the United States, as a great world power, beyond the confines of the Western Hemisphere, ignorant of the bearing of this step upon the national interest and guided by moral principles which are completely divorced from the national interest. When at the end of the Spanish-American War the status of the Philippines had to be determined, McKinley expected and found no guidance in the traditional national interests of the United States. According to his own testimony, he knelt beside his bed in prayer, and in the wee hours of the morning he heard the voice of God telling him—as was to be expected —to annex the Philippines.

This period initiated by McKinley, in which moral principles no longer justify the enduring national interest as in the second, but replace it as a guide for action, finds its fulfillment in the political thought of Woodrow Wilson. Wilson's thought not only disregards the national interest, but is explicitly opposed to it on moral grounds. "It is a very perilous thing," he said in his address at Mobile on October 27, 1913,

> to determine the foreign policy of a nation in the terms of
> material interest. It not only is unfair to those with whom
> you are dealing, but it is degrading as regards your own
> actions. . . . We dare not turn from the principle that
> morality and not expediency is the thing that must guide
> us, and that we will never condone iniquity because it is
> most convenient to do so.

Wilson's war-time speeches are but an elaboration of this
philosophy. An excerpt from his address of September 27, 1918,
opening the campaign for the Fourth Liberty Loan, will suffice
to show the continuity of that philosophy:

> It is of capital importance that we should also be explicitly
> agreed that no peace shall be obtained by any kind of com-
> promise or abatement of the principles we have avowed as
> the principles for which we are fighting. . . .
> First, the impartial justice meted out must involve no dis-
> crimination between those to whom we wish to be just and
> those to whom we do not wish to be just. It must be a justice
> that plays no favorites and knows no standard but the equal
> rights of the several peoples concerned;
> Second, no special or separate interest of any single nation
> or any group of nations can be made the basis of any part of
> the settlement which is not consistent with the common
> interest of all;
> Third, there can be no leagues or alliances or special cov-
> enants and understandings within the general and common
> family of the League of Nations;
> Fourth, and more specifically, there can be no special,
> selfish economic combinations within the League and no
> employment of any form of economic boycott or exclusion
> except as the power of economic penalty by exclusion from
> the markets of the world may be vested in the League of

Nations itself as a means of discipline and control.

Fifth, all international agreements and treaties of every kind must be made known in their entirety to the rest of the world.

Special alliances and economic rivalries and hostilities have been the prolific source in the modern world of the plans and passions that produce war. It would be an insincere as well as insecure peace that did not exclude them in definite and binding terms. . . .

National purposes have fallen more and more into the background and the common purpose of enlightened mankind has taken their place. The counsels of plain men have become on all hands more simple and straightforward and more unified than the counsels of sophisticated men of affairs, who still retain the impression that they are playing a game of power and playing for high stakes. That is why I have said that this is a peoples' war, not a statesmen's. Statesmen must follow the clarified common thought or be broken.

Yet in his political actions, especially under the pressure of the First World War, Wilson could no more than Jefferson before him discount completely the national interest of the United States. Wilson's case, however, was different from Jefferson's in two respects. For one, Wilson was never able, even when the national interest of the United States was directly menaced, to conceive of the danger in other than moral terms. It was only the objective force of the national interest, which no rational man could escape, that imposed upon him as the object of his moral indignation the source of America's mortal danger. Thus in 1917 Wilson led the United States into war against Germany for the same reasons, only half-known to himself, for which Jefferson had wished and worked alternately for the victory of England and of France. Germany threatened the balance of power in Europe, and it was in order to remove that threat—and not to make the world safe for democracy—that the United States put its weight into the Allies' scale. Wilson pursued the right policy, but he pursued it for the wrong reasons.

Not only did the crusading fervor of moral reformation obliterate the awareness of the United States' traditional interest in the maintenance of the European balance of power, to be accomplished through the defeat of Germany. Wilson's moral fervor also had politically disastrous effects, for which there is no precedent in the history of the United States. Wilson's moral objective required the destruction of the Kaiser's autocracy, and this happened also to be required by the political interests of the United States. The political interests of the United States required, beyond this immediate objective of total victory, the restoration of the European balance of power, traditional guarantor of American security. Yet it was in indignation at the moral deficiencies of that very balance of power, "forever discredited," as he thought, that Wilson had asked the American people to take up arms against the Central Powers! Once military victory had put an end to the immediate threat to American security, the very logic of his moral position—let us remember that consistency is the moralist's supreme virtue—drove him toward substituting for the concrete national interest of the United States the general postulate of a brave new world where the national interest of the United States, as that of all other nations, would disappear in a community of interests comprising mankind.

Consequently, Wilson considered it to be the purpose of victory not to restore a new, viable balance of power, but to make an end to it once and forever. "You know," he told the English people at Manchester on December 30, 1918,

that the United States has always felt from the very beginning of her history that she must keep herself separate from any kind of connection with European politics, and I want to say very frankly to you that she is not now interested in European politics. But she is interested in the partnership of right between America and Europe. If the future

had nothing for us but a new attempt to keep the w
a right poise by a balance of power, the United States
take no interest, because she will join no combinat
power which is not the combination of all of us. She is not
interested merely in the peace of Europe, but in the peace
of the world.

Faced with the national interests of the great allied powers,
Wilson had nothing to oppose or support them with but his moral
principles, with the result that the neglect of the American national interest was not compensated for by the triumph of political
morality. In the end Wilson had to consent to a series of uneasy
compromises which were a betrayal of his moral principles—for
principles can, by their very nature, not be made the object of
compromise—and which satisfied nobody's national aspirations.
These compromises had no relation at all to the traditional American national interest in a viable European balance of power.
Thus Wilson returned from Versailles a compromised idealist, an
empty-handed statesman, a discredited ally. In that triple failure
lies the tragedy not only of Wilson, a great yet misguided man,
but of Wilsonianism as a political doctrine as well.

14. ROBERT E. OSGOOD: THE NATIONALISTIC DEFECTION FROM WILSON'S PROGRAM

*Robert E. Osgood is associated with the Center for the Study of
American Foreign Policy at the University of Chicago. In his
writings he has been particularly interested to explain how American attitudes and conceptions have affected and limited our
foreign policy, and his books have marked him as one of the
most productive scholars in the field of international politics. The*

Reprinted from pages 283 to 286, 303 to 304 from *Ideals and Self-Interest in America's
Foreign Relations* by Robert E. Osgood, by permission of The University of Chicago
Press. Copyright 1953. The University of Chicago Press.

following selection is taken from IDEALS AND SELF-INTER-EST IN AMERICA'S FOREIGN RELATIONS. As you read it, try to answer the following questions:

1. What, in Osgood's opinion, had Wilson forgotten about American public attitudes toward the war?
2. Why did Wilson's peace program arouse so much opposition in the United States? What were the viewpoints of such opponents as Theodore Roosevelt and Senators Lodge and Borah?
3. Does Osgood think that Wilson's ideals were incompatible with America's vital national interests?

Woodrow Wilson viewed the making of peace as a fulfilment of the purpose for which America had waged war, and he relied upon the common people of America, with their tremendous resources of idealism, to support his plans for peace with the same zeal they had spent upon war. On the day of the Armistice, November 11, 1918, he told a joint session of Congress that victory was no mere military decision, no mere relief from the trials of war, but a divine vindication of universal principles and a call to greater duties ahead. Two days before he sailed for the Paris peace conference he proclaimed the continuation in peace of America's disinterested service to humanity during war: "We are about to give order and organization to this peace not only for ourselves but for the other peoples of the world as well, so far as they will suffer us to serve them. It is international justice that we seek, not domestic safety merely."

Wilson forgot—if, indeed, he ever realized it—that America, as a whole, had not entered the war in the spirit of altruism; that there was implicit in American intervention no acceptance of revolutionary international commitments; that the nation's war-born enthusiasm for a world made safe for democracy and the end of all wars gained a good part of its inspiration from a simple desire to lick the Hun and stay out of future trouble. However fervent America's belief in the righteousness of its cause may have been, the general approval of Wilson's war aims implied no eagerness to sacrifice traditional modes of national conduct for the sake of other nations and peoples.

Nevertheless, one cannot deny that the American people had come to believe that their war was a crusade for a freer, more democratic, and more peaceful world. This vague aspiration would somehow have to be fulfilled in order to justify the sacrifices of war. For by the time the German Army was defeated, the principal reasons which had justified intervention in April, 1917—the maintenance of neutral rights and the vindication of national honor—had all but disappeared from popular discussion. The war had been fought for a different set of reasons from those that had led to intervention; and these reasons, however imperfectly conceived, raised expectations of a nature that could not be satisfied by mere military victory.

Wilson counted upon the fundamental altruism of the people to bridge the gap between the League and tradition. But with the strongest basis for popular idealism removed by victory, it seems likely that only some persuasive appeal to fundamental national self-interest could have sustained America's crusade into the period of peacemaking. Yet Wilson, by his very nature, could appeal only for an even greater subordination of self-interest to moral principle.

Wilson insisted that the League of Nations was pre-eminently a moral conception, an organization to turn the "searching light of conscience" upon wrong and aggression wherever it might be contemplated. It followed from his faith in the moral sense of the masses that the American people were bound to embrace this plan once they understood its lofty nature. Therefore, he expounded its transcendent idealism in the confidence that Americans would prefer the interests of mankind to all other interests. While this approach made American membership in an international league seem less and less compelling to the great body of Americans as war-born idealism subsided, it positively assured a mounting hostility toward the project on the part of Realistic national egoists like Roosevelt and Lodge.

Although Wilson was not ignorant of the practical national advantages to be gained through membership in a league, his whole nature rebelled at a frank acknowledgment of expediency as a basis for national action. He preferred to emphasize the universal moral principles that bound men together as human beings rather than the fine adjustments of self-interest among nations, which might disintegrate into violent jealousies with a slight change of circumstance. Consequently, he presented the League as a substitute for the balance-of-power system, not as a supplementation or extension of it. As he told an English audience on December 30, "If the future had nothing for us but a new attempt to keep the world at a right poise by a balance of power, the United States would take no interest, because she will join no combination of power which is not the combination of all of us."

Roosevelt, on the other hand, took just the opposite view. In his opinion it was folly to join a concert of nations that did not reflect the actual power situation. As far as he was concerned, both practical and idealistic considerations pointed to the wisdom of an Anglo-American alliance. On November 19 he wrote Arthur Lee that he had become more convinced than ever that "there should be the closest alliance between the British Empire and the United States." To George Haven Putnam, who had solicited his membership in the English-Speaking Union, he wrote,

> I regard the British Navy as probably the most potent instrumentality for peace in the world. . . . Moreover, I am now prepared to say what five years ago I would not have said. I think the time has come when the United States and the British Empire can agree to a universal arbitration treaty.

In one of his last editorials Roosevelt declared that he strongly shared the feeling that there should be some kind of international league to prevent a recurrence of war, but he warned his readers not to be deceived by sham idealism, by high-sounding and meaningless phrases, such as those embodied in the Fourteen Points. Let us face the facts, he wrote. The first fact is that nations are not equal. Therefore, let us limit the league to the present Allies and admit others only as their conduct warrants it. Let us specifically reserve certain rights from the jurisdiction of any international body. America should be very careful about promising to interfere with, or on behalf of, "impotent or disorderly nations and peoples outside this league" where they lie "wholly outside our sphere of interest." Roosevelt concluded with a plea for universal military training.

Actually, Roosevelt's conception of a peace settlement as one phase of a continuing accommodation of power was as remote from the popular view as Wilson's vision of the selfless submerging of national sovereignty in a community of interest. Both views involved a serious break with traditional conceptions of America's relation to world politics. However, in his strong assertion of national prerogatives Roosevelt was joined by parochial nationalists, such as Borah and Beveridge, who were unalterably opposed to all involvements in power politics, including those for limited national ends, on the grounds that nothing that happened overseas could be of enough concern to the United States to warrant contaminating the nation by association with the evil balance-of-power system. While Lodge and Roosevelt had never been opposed to joining an international organization that would redound to the national interest, Beveridge and Borah were convinced, as a matter of principle, that the national interest and membership in a league were mutually contradictory. But, whatever their differences, both groups were agreed that American interests came first; and, if only for this reason, Wilson's persistent association of the League with altruism proved as repelling to realistic as to parochial nationalists.

Moreover, the President's moralistic approach gave the nationalists a distinct tactical advantage in the debate over the terms of America's membership in the League; for if America's entrance into the League of Nations were purely a philanthropic gesture, then there was strength in the argument that the nation ought to be able to determine, independently of others, the proper extent of its own generosity. On this basis Lodge argued for his reservations to the League Covenant. In an address before the Senate on February 28, 1919, he accepted Wilson's contention that American participation in the League would be almost wholly for the benefit of others and asserted that, therefore, the United States had a right to limit the sacrifice of its sovereignty as it pleased. On August 12 he argued, "Surely it is not too much to insist that when we are offered nothing but the opportunity to give and to aid others we should have the right to say what sacrifices we shall make and what the magnitude of our gifts should be."

Senator Borah had presented the same thesis of limited philanthropy the week before.

> I may be willing to help my neighbor, though he be improvident or unfortunate, but I do not necessarily want him for a business partner. I may be willing to give liberally of my means, of my council and advice, even of my strength or blood, to protect his family from attack or injustice, but I do not want him placed in a position where he may decide for me when and how I shall act or to what extent I shall make sacrifice.

If the majority of the nation were willing to grant philanthropy a greater scope than Borah, it was not because they were more idealistic but simply because they were less apprehensive of the sacrifice demanded of them.

*   *   *

It must be said that President Wilson's leadership throughout the period of war and peacemaking, though it was eternally right in its moral objectives, could not have been deliberately calculated to defeat its own ends more surely; for by exhorting his countrymen to subordinate their self-interest to abstract moral

standards and the welfare of the rest of the world, Wilson demanded an impossible and an unnecessary performance, encouraged the postwar repudiation of the very objects he sought,
and obscured the one basis upon which a more realistic view of
national conduct could have been created, a basis which might
have recommended itself to nationalists and internationalists,
egoists and idealists alike. That basis was enlightened self-interest.

Nevertheless, it would be a serious distortion of the evolution
of America's international conduct to imply that President Wilson could have done much to create a popular awareness of the
realistic basis for judging the League issue; for the whole climate
of opinion resisted any such awareness, and Wilson did not have
it within his power to work any fundamental change in the
American attitude toward world politics, even though he might
well have secured American membership in the League of Nations. If an appeal to altruism merely intensified the nation's
shocked innocence and the tenacity of its desire for isolation,
what self-interested motives could have inspired a realistic awareness of the political consequences of national action? Not the
urge to assert American power aggressively; Americans had rejected this motive soon after their first crusade. Not the instinct
of self-preservation, for the circumstances of international relations simply did not press upon the United States in such a way
as to excite fear for survival.

World War I demonstrated once more the power of America's
faith in its ideals. The abiding aspiration for world peace and
international harmony, for democracy and the elimination of
tyranny, for the promotion of humanitarianism and material welfare, for the abolition of oppression and poverty among all peoples; these ideals were no flimsy rationalization of war-born
patriotism; they were rooted too solidly in American tradition.
Moreover, the rest of the world generally recognized the strength
and the sincerity of American idealism and for this reason wel-
comed American leadership as a breath of hope and enlighten-
ment in the troubled society of nations. In spite of the bitterness

toward Woodrow Wilson and America, which festered in the unwholesome environment of postwar Europe, the United States had enjoyed an unparalleled reputation for idealism among foreign peoples; America's desertion of its crusade in 1919–20 was a severe blow to them.

Could it be that ideals which carried such weight in the world as these were incompatible with America's vital interests? On the contrary, the course of events in the period between two world wars suggests that there was a vast area in which American ideals and American interests coincided; indeed, in which they were indispensable to one another. The popular realization of this fact and the will to act upon it realistically was born in the adversity of a second world war. The interim of precarious peace between the crusade for democracy and the fight for survival was a fitting prelude to this transformation.

15. ARTHUR S. LINK: WILSON AND THE LIBERAL PEACE PROGRAM

Arthur S. Link of Princeton University is writing what promises to be the definitive biography of Woodrow Wilson for years to come. Three volumes of this work have already been completed and, although the volume on the problems of war and peace in Wilson's second administration has not yet appeared, Professor Link has already presented his general pattern of interpretation in the Albert Shaw Lectures in Diplomatic History, delivered at The Johns Hopkins University in 1956. The following selection is taken from the published version of those lectures, entitled WILSON THE DIPLOMATIST. Read the excerpt and consider these questions:

From Arthur S. Link, *Wilson the Diplomatist* (c. 1957, The Johns Hopkins Press), pp. 109–125. Reprinted with permission.

1. What major concessions did Wilson have to make to the other allied powers at the Peace Conference?
2. Was Wilson able to win any concessions from the French, British, Italians, and Japanese?
3. What does Link think about the wisdom of Wilson's efforts regarding the political and territorial arrangements in central and eastern Europe?
4. Why does Link believe that Wilson "arrived intuitively at the right answers" concerning Bolshevik Russia, while his "Allied conferees" with their more "realistic" understanding "arrived at the wrong ones"?
5. How does Link assess Wilson's efforts at Paris? Would you add up the box score of Wilson's successes and failures in the same way?

. . . It is not my purpose here either to write a biography of Wilson during this period or another history of the Paris Peace Conference. Indeed, to tell the story in all its detail would be to obscure my objective in the balance of this lecture. That objective, simply stated, is to determine the degree to which Wilson succeeded or failed in vindicating the liberal peace program. This can best be done by describing the crucial areas of disagreement and by showing what the outcome was when Wilsonian idealism clashed with Allied ambitions.

The overshadowing necessity of the Paris conference was the devising of plans and measures to assure security for the French against future German aggression. Wilson offered safety in the hope of a Reich reformed because it was democratic, and in a League of Nations that would provide the machinery for preventing any aggression in the future. To the French, whose territory had been twice invaded by the Germans in less than half a century and who were still inferior in manpower and industry to their eastern neighbor, such promises were not enough. Having lived under the shadow of the German colossus, they were determined to destroy it and by so doing to assure a peaceful Europe. Thus Georges Clemenceau, the French Premier, following plans devised by Marshal Foch and approved even before the United States entered the war, proposed to tear the west bank of the Rhine from Germany by the creation of one or more autonomous Rhenish republics under French control.

Arguing that the dismemberment of Germany in the West would outrageously violate the Pre-Armistice Agreement and create a wound on the body of the world community that would fester for generations to come, Wilson opposed this plan with grim determination during long and violent debates with the French spokesmen. The tension reached a climax during late March and early April, 1919, when Clemenceau accused Wilson of being pro-German and the President ordered his ship, the *George Washington,* to prepare to take him back to the United States. Some agreement, obviously, was a compelling necessity; without it the conference would have failed entirely, and the French would have been at liberty to execute their own plans in their own way.

In the showdown it was the French who made the vital concessions, by yielding their demands for the creation of the Rhenish republics and the permanent French occupation of the Rhineland. In return, Wilson and David Lloyd George, the British Prime Minister, who gave the President important support on this issue, agreed to permit a fifteen-year occupation of the Rhineland and signed with Clemenceau treaties promising that the United States and Great Britain would come to the aid of France if she were attacked by Germany. These concessions saved the conference from actual disruption. Coupled with provisions for the permanent demilitarization of the west bank of the Rhine and a strip along the east bank, and for severe limitations upon German land forces, the guarantee treaties afforded such security as the French were determined to achieve.

A second issue, that of reparations and indemnities, evoked perhaps the most protracted debates at the conference and the most lasting bitterness afterward. In cynical disregard of the Pre-Armistice Agreement, which stipulated that Germany should be liable for civilian damages, Clemenceau and Lloyd George demanded that she be made to shoulder the entire costs of the war to the Allied peoples. In the face of an aroused British and French public opinion and heavy pressure by their leaders,

Wilson made perhaps his most conspicuous concessions at Paris. First, he agreed that Germany should be forced to bear the costs of disability pensions to Allied veterans and their families, on the ground that these were really civilian damages. Second, he approved the inclusion of Article 231 in the treaty, by which Germany and her allies were forced to accept responsibility for all Allied war losses and damages, although this responsibility was actually limited to civilian damages in Article 232. Third, he agreed that the French should have the right to occupy the Rhineland beyond the stipulated period if the Germans failed to meet their reparations obligations. In addition, the President consented to the immediate Allied seizure of some $5 billion worth of German property; French ownership of the coal mines in the Saar Valley, as compensation for the wanton destruction wrought in France by the retreating German army; and French occupation of the Saar under the supervision of the League of Nations for twenty years.

Actually, the concessions that Wilson made would not have mattered much if he had succeeded in winning the crucial point for which he and his financial advisers fought so hard. It was the proposal that a Reparations Commission be established to fix a schedule of reparations payments to be made for a definite period, the amount to be determined, not upon the basis of Allied hopes, but upon the basis of Germany's capacity to pay. Under the American plan, moreover, the Commission might reduce or cancel reparations payments altogether if they proved to be more than the German economy could sustain.

In the controversy that ensued the British were badly divided, but they finally veered toward the American position. But on April 5, 1919, just at the time when it seemed that the American plan might prevail, Colonel House (speaking for the ailing President) surrendered unconditionally to the French demands, by agreeing that the Reparations Commission should be instructed only to compute the reparations bill and to enforce its complete payment, without any reference to a definite period or to Germany's capacity to pay. It was a disastrous instance of yielding, for it bound the President to the French position and guaranteed that the reparations settlement would embitter international relations until statesmen finally admitted that it had been a fiasco from the beginning.

A third issue, one that threatened to disrupt the conference almost before it could begin, was the question of the disposition of the former German colonies, all of which had been occupied by Allied forces during the war. In the Fourteen Points Wilson had called for an "absolutely impartial adjustment of all colonial claims" with due regard for the interests of the peoples involved. As he explained during preconference discussions in London in December, 1918, what he had in mind was to make the former German colonies the common property of the League and to have them governed by small nations under specific international mandate and supervision. In pressing for this objective, he ran head-on into commitments for annexation that the British government had made to the dominions and to Japan, and into an absolutely stubborn determination on the part of the latter that these promises should be honored.

The issue was fought out during the opening days of the Paris conference, with Wilson alone arrayed against Lloyd George and the spokesmen of the dominions and of Japan. At no time, it is important to note, did the President envisage the return of the disputed colonies to Germany, for he agreed with most experts who accused the Germans of being oppressive and exploitative masters. (This opinion is still held by most specialists in the field of colonial administration.) Wilson, moreover, soon abandoned his plan for mandating the colonies to small nations, on the ground that it was impractical, and accepted the necessity of a division on a basis of occupation. But he refused to yield the chief objective for which he fought, the clear establishment of the principle that the governments to which the former German possessions were awarded should hold those colonies under the specific mandate and supervision of the League for the benefit of the native peoples affected and of the entire world. This was a notable victory, perhaps more notable than Wilson himself realized, because the establishment of the mandate system spelled the eventual doom of colonialism, not merely in the mandates, but throughout the entire world.

Wilson suffered momentary defeat, however, on the closely related issue of Japanese rights in the Shantung Province of China, a matter infinitely more complicated than the disposition of the German colonies because it involved the entire balance of power in the Far East. The Japanese had entered the war in 1914, captured the German naval base at Kiaochow, China, and overrun the entire German concession in the Shantung Province. They had proceeded afterward, from 1915 to 1917, to impose treaties upon the Chinese government recognizing their rights as successors to Germany in the province and to win a similar recognition from the foreign offices in London, Paris, and Petrograd. Legally, therefore, the Japanese claims at the Paris conference were nearly impregnable.

But technical legalities carried little weight with the man who was fighting to help the Chinese people recover a lost province and to avert the danger of Japanese domination of northern China; and with almost incredible effrontery Wilson set out to vindicate the principle of self-determination. He presented the Chinese delegates to the conference, so that they could plead their own case. He appealed to sentiments and principles with unrivaled eloquence, urging the Japanese to make their contribution to a better world by foregoing conquest. Only after it was indelibly clear that the Japanese would sign no treaty that did not recognize their claims did Wilson withdraw his pressure. In agreeing to recognize Japan's right to the former concession, however, the President won verbal promises that full sovereignty in the Shantung Province would be restored to China, a pledge the Japanese later honored.

A fifth issue, the question of Italian claims to former parts of the Austro-Hungarian Empire, provoked the bitterest personal acrimony at the Paris conference. In line with their national traditions, the Italians had bargained astutely with both alliances in 1914 and 1915 and had entered the war against the Central Powers in the latter year under the terms of the Treaty of London, by which the Allies had promised the Italians the Austrian Trentino to the Brenner Pass, the district of Trieste, the Dalmatian coast below the port of Fiume, and other territories.

There would have been no great conflict at Paris over this matter if the Italians had succeeded in keeping their appetites within reasonable bounds. Following the detailed interpretation of the Fourteen Points prepared by Frank Cobb and Walter Lippmann of The Inquiry in October, 1918, Wilson conceded Italy's claim to the Trentino on strategic grounds even before the peace conference opened, although he perhaps later regretted this concession when he realized the degree to which it violated the principle of self-determination. Nor did he object to the Italian claims to Trieste, which were in accord with the Fourteen Points, even though they had been confirmed in the kind of diplomatic bargaining that he detested most.

Conflict between Wilson and the Italian Prime Minister and Foreign Minister, Vittorio Orlando and Sidney Sonnino, arose chiefly because the latter, not satisfied with their more or less legitimate fruits of victory, demanded also the Adriatic port of Fiume, which had been awarded to the South Slavs by the Treaty of London and would be the only good outlet to the sea for the new state of Yugoslavia. By thus overreaching themselves, the Italians alienated their British and French friends and gave Wilson a strategic opportunity that he quickly exploited. In brief, he capitalized upon the weakness of the Italian claim to Fiume to justify a sweeping denial of the Italian right to the Dalmatian coast and, through it, complete control of the Adriatic.

The climax of the grueling battle came on April 23, 1919, when Wilson, sick of making futile pleas to the masters of the old diplomacy, appealed over their heads directly to the Italian people. In a gigantic bluff Orlando and Sonnino left the conference, only to return in early May after it was evident that the President would not yield. There then ensued the most incredible negotiations of the entire conference and a final recognition that the peacemakers could not agree upon the Fiume and Adriatic issues. They were left for settlement by the League of Nations and by direct negotiations between Italy and Yugoslavia.

Four other great issues before the Paris conferees were no less important than the ones we have discussed, but it will serve our purposes here merely to describe the role that Wilson played in helping to find solutions for them.

First, there was the business of redeeming the promise, made by all the belligerents during the war, to establish an independent Poland. The only controversies of any consequence about this matter involved the disposition of the port of Danzig and the German province of Upper Silesia. In both disputes Wilson joined Lloyd George in standing firm against Polish and French demands and in winning the internationalization of Danzig and a plebiscite to determine how Upper Silesia should be partitioned between Germany and Poland.

Second, there was the necessity of deciding the fate of the component remains of the Austro-Hungarian Empire. Wilson's role in this matter has been gravely misunderstood and distorted, especially by certain British critics who have ascribed to him virtually full responsibility for the destruction of the Empire. This is an exaggeration worthy of the good Baron Munchausen. Before the summer of 1918, Wilson had demanded the federalization, not the breaking up, of the realms of the Hapsburgs. Their Empire had already been destroyed from within by centrifugal forces even before Wilson, in the late summer of 1918, specifically amended the Fourteen Points by recognizing the new state of Czechoslovakia and by thus endorsing the idea of breaking up the Austro-Hungarian Empire. By the time that the Paris Peace Conference assembled the new states of Central Europe existed in fact. They would have been created, and their leaders would have demanded the right of self-determination even though Wilson had never uttered that magic word. All that Wilson or anyone else at Paris, for that matter, could do was to try to draw the least absurd boundary lines possible and to impose arrangements to preserve some degree of economic unity in Central Europe.

Third, there was the even more perplexing necessity of dealing with a chaotic and changing situation in Russia. It is true, as one scholar has recently pointed out, that Wilson's notions about the capacities of the Russian people for effective self-government and self-determination, expressed in Point 6, were romantic. It is also true that he had only a vague understanding of the character of the international communist movement. Yet in spite of it all he arrived intuitively at the right answers, while his Allied conferees, with all their superior knowledge and more "realistic" understanding, arrived at the wrong ones.

In all the inter-Allied discussions about Russia before and during the peace conference, Wilson defended two propositions —first, that the Russian people must be permitted to solve their internal problems without outside intervention, and, second, that communism was a revolutionary answer to egregious wrongs and could be met only by removing its root causes, not by force. As he put it, "In my opinion, trying to stop a revolutionary movement by troops in the field is like using a broom to hold back a great ocean."

Wilson acted throughout in accord with these assumptions. During 1918 he resisted heavy Allied pressure for a general anti-Bolshevik intervention. Finally yielding to what seemed to be military and humane necessities, he sent American troops to Archangel and Vladivostok, but only for specific purposes, not for general political intervention in the Russian Civil War, and only in small numbers and for the briefest time possible, as if to chaperone Allied conduct in these areas. At the peace conference, moreover, he again resisted all British and French suggestions for intervention in Russia proper and even refused to send American troops to Vienna to help halt what seemed to be an onrushing Bolshevik tide. The British and particularly the

French executed their own far-reaching military interventions at this time and later, to be sure, but Wilson was in no way responsible for these fiascos.

Fourth, there was the issue of disarmament, the key, Wilson believed, to peace and security in the future. What the President proposed was that the victors accept virtually the same limitations that they were imposing upon the Germans, by agreeing in the peace treaty itself to abolish conscription, prohibit private manufacture of the implements of war, and maintain armies sufficient only to preserve domestic order and fulfill international obligations. What Wilson encountered was insuperable opposition from the French; what he won, only a vague promise to undertake general disarmament in the future. Perhaps because he made so little progress toward the limitation of land forces, he never seriously proposed naval disarmament at the conference.

We come now to the one issue that took precedence over all the others in Wilson's plans and purposes—the question of the League of Nations, which I mention last because it was so pervasively involved in all the discussions at Paris. There were two divergent concepts of what the League should be and do that cast a revealing light upon the motives and objectives of opposing forces at Paris. One was the French concept of a league of victors, which would be used to guarantee French military domination of the Continent. Embodied in a draft presented at the first meeting of the League of Nations Commission on February 3, 1919, the French plan envisaged the creation of an international army and a general staff with startling supranational powers. The other was Wilson's concept of a league of all nations, the vanquished as well as the victors, in short, a universal alliance for the purpose of creating a concert of power, not really a supranational agency, but one depending upon the leadership of the great powers, the co-operation of sovereign states, and the organized opinion of mankind for its effectiveness.

With strong British support Wilson had his way easily enough in the meetings of the commission that drafted the Covenant, or constitution, of the League. The crucial conflicts came during the discussions of the Council of Ten and the Big Four, when the French, Italians, Japanese, and even the British at times relentlessly used the threat of refusing to support Wilson's League as a way of exacting concessions on other issues. Time and again Wilson did retreat, but by thus yielding he won the larger goal, a League of Nations constructed almost exactly as he wanted it, the Covenant of which was firmly embedded in all the treaties signed at Paris.

That Covenant was a treaty binding its signatory members in an alliance of nonaggression and friendship and creating the machinery for international co-operation in many fields and for the prevention of war. The heart of the Covenant was embodied in Article 10, which read as follows:

> The Members of the League undertake to respect and preserve as against external aggression the territorial integrity and existing political independence of all Members of the League. In case of any such aggression or in case of any threat or danger of such aggression the Council shall advise upon the means by which this obligation shall be fulfilled.

The structure erected was the League itself, an international parliament with an Assembly in which all members were represented and an executive Council in which the great powers shared a greater responsibility with a minority of smaller states. In addition, there was a judicial branch—a Permanent Court of International Justice, and an administrative arm—a Secretariat and various commissions charged with responsibility for executing the peace treaties and for promoting international co-operation in economic and social fields. It was, Wilson said when he first presented the Covenant to a full session of the conference, "a living thing . . ., a definite guarantee of peace . . . against the things which have just come near bringing the whole structure of civilization into ruin."

Did Wilson fail at Paris? This is a question that has been asked and answered a thousand times by statesmen and scholars since the Versailles Treaty was signed in 1919. It will be asked so long as men remember Woodrow Wilson and the world's first major effort to solve the problem of recurring wars. The answer that one gives depends not only upon the circumstances and mood prevailing at the time it is given, but as well upon the view that one takes of history and of the potentialities and limitations of human endeavor. That is to say, it makes a great deal of difference whether one judges Wilson's work by certain absolute so-called moral standards, or whether one views what he did remembering the obstacles that he faced, the pressures under which he labored, the things that were possible and impossible to achieve at the time, and what would have happened had he not been present at the conference.

I should perhaps begin my own assessment by saying that the Versailles Treaty, measured by the standards that Wilson had enunciated from 1916 to 1919, obviously failed to fulfill entirely the liberal peace program. It was not, as Wilson had demanded in his Peace without Victory speech and implicitly promised in the Fourteen Points, a peace among equals. It was, rather, as the Germans contended then and later, a *diktat* imposed by victors upon a beaten foe. It shouldered Germany with a reparations liability that was both economically difficult to satisfy and politically a source of future international conflict. It satisfied the victors' demands for a division of the enemy's colonies and territories. In several important instances it violated the principle of self-determination. Finally, it was filled with pin pricks, like the provision for the trial of the former German Emperor, that served no purpose except to humiliate the German people. It does not, therefore, require much argument to prove that Wilson failed to win the settlement that he had demanded and that the Allies had promised in the Pre-Armistice Agreement.

To condemn Wilson because he failed in part is, however, to miss the entire moral of the story of Versailles. That moral is a simple one: The Paris peace settlement reveals more clearly than any other episode of the twentieth century the tension between the ideal and the real in history and the truth of the proposition that failure inheres in all human striving. It does not make much sense merely to list Wilson's failures. We can see their meaning only when we understand *why* he failed as he did.

Wilson failed at Paris not because he did not fight with all his mind and strength for the whole of the liberal peace program. Never before in his career had he fought more tenaciously or pleaded more eloquently. Nor did he fail because, as John Maynard Keynes and Harold Nicholson have portrayed him in their unkind caricatures, he was incompetent, uninformed, and "bamboozled" by men of superior wit and learning. Indeed, after reading the records of the deliberations at Paris one cannot escape the feeling that Wilson was the best informed and on the whole the wisest man among the Big Four.

Wilson failed as he did because his handicaps and the obstacles against which he fought made failure inevitable. In the first place, he had lost most of his strategic advantages by the time that the peace conference opened. German military power, upon which he had relied as a balance against Allied ambitions, was now totally gone. Wilson had no power of coercion over Britain and France, for they were no longer dependent upon American manpower and resources for survival. His only recourse, withdrawal from the conference, would have been utterly fatal to his program. It would have meant inevitably a Carthaginian peace imposed by the French, as the British alone could never have prevented the French from carrying out their plans to destroy Germany. In these circumstances, therefore, compromise was not merely a necessity, but a compelling necessity to avert (from Wilson's point of view) a far worse alternative.

In contrast to the strength of the French were Wilson's other weaknesses. His claim to the right to speak in the name of the American people had been seriously weakened by the election of a Republican Congress in November, 1918, and was denied during the peace conference itself by Republican leaders like

Senator Henry Cabot Lodge. In addition, there was the failure of Colonel House, upon whom Wilson had relied as his strong right arm, to support liberal peace ideals during that period of the conference when House was still the President's spokesman. House was so eager for harmony that he was willing to yield to almost any demand and on several crucial occasions seriously undercut and compromised the President.

Another of Wilson's obstacles, namely, the character of his antagonists at Paris, has often been overlooked. Clemenceau, Lloyd George, Orlando, Baron Sonnino, and the Japanese delegates were all tough and resourceful negotiators, masters of the game of diplomacy, quick to seize every advantage that the less experienced American offered.

To overcome such opposition Wilson had at his command the threat of withdrawal, the promise of American support for the right kind of settlement and of leadership in the League of Nations, and the fact that he did speak for liberal groups not only in his own country, but throughout the world as well. These were sources of considerable strength, to be sure, but they were not enough to enable Wilson to impose his own settlement.

In spite of it all Wilson did succeed in winning a settlement that honored more of the Fourteen Points—not to mention the additional thirteen points—than it violated and in large measure vindicated his liberal ideals. There was the restoration of Belgium, the return of Alsace-Lorraine to France, and the creation of an independent Poland with access to the sea. There was the satisfaction of the claims of the Central European and Balkan peoples to self-determination. There was the at least momentary destruction of German military power. Most important, there was the fact that the Paris settlement provided machinery for its own revision through the League of Nations and the hope that the passing of time and American leadership in the League would help to heal the world's wounds and build a future free from fear.

As it turned out, many of Wilson's expectations were fulfilled

even though the American people refused to play the part assigned to them. For example, the reparations problem was finally
solved in the 1920's in a way not dissimilar from the method that
Wilson had proposed. Germany was admitted to the League in
1926, and that organization ceased to be a mere league of victors.
Effective naval disarmament was accomplished in 1921 and 1930.
Even the great and hitherto elusive goal of land disarmament
and the recognition of Germany's right to military equality was
being seriously sought by international action in the early 1930's.
In brief, the Paris settlement, in spite of its imperfections, did
create a new international order that functioned well, relatively
speaking. And it failed, not because it was imperfect, but because it was not defended when challenges arose in the 1930's.

Thus I conclude by suggesting that for Woodrow Wilson the
Paris Peace Conference was more a time of heroic striving and
impressive achievement than of failure. By fighting against odds
that would have caused weaker men to surrender, he was able
to prevent the Carthaginian kind of peace that we have seen
to our regret in our own time; and he was able to create the
machinery for the gradual attainment of the kind of settlement
that he would have liked to impose at once. The Paris settlement,
therefore, was not inevitably a "lost peace." It could have been,
rather, the foundation of a viable and secure world order and
therefore a lasting memorial to its chief architect, if only the
victors had maintained the will to enforce what Wilson signed.

Now that you have completed the readings in this volume, write a paper on these final questions: *Did Wilson fail at Paris? Were his ideas of peacemaking too idealistic and moralistic? Did he demand a greater sacrifice of national interests than the people of America and Europe could give, or did he point the way toward the kind of international order that was indispensable in the changing conditions of the twentieth century?* Be sure to defend your judgment with a clear-cut analysis of Wilson's successes and failures. If you wish to write a longer paper on this problem, the following books should be helpful.

Part 5

Conclusion

SUGGESTED BIBLIOGRAPHY

I. PEACE CONFERENCE: 1919—CONTEMPORARIES

Ray Stannard Baker, *Woodrow Wilson and the World Settlement.* 3 vols., 1922

David Lloyd George, *Memoirs of the Peace Conference.* 2 vols., 1939

André Tardieu, *The Truth About the Treaty.* 1921

John Maynard Keynes, *The Economic Consequences of the Peace.* 1920

Étienne Mantoux, *The Carthaginian Peace, or the Economic Consequences of Mr. Keynes.* 1946

Harold Nicholson, *Peacemaking, 1919.* 1933

Robert Lansing, *The Peace Negotiations.* 1921

II. WILSON—BIOGRAPHIES AND CRITIQUES

Ray Stannard Baker, *Woodrow Wilson: Life and Letters*. 6 vols., 1927–1937.

Arthur S. Link, *Woodrow Wilson: The Road to the White House.* 1947

———. *Woodrow Wilson: The New Freedom.* 1956

———. *Woodrow Wilson: The Struggle for Neutrality 1914–1915.* 1960

John M. Blum, *Woodrow Wilson, and the Politics of Morality.* 1956

Harley Notter, *The Origins of the Foreign Policy of Woodrow Wilson.* 1937

Arthur S. Link, *Wilson the Diplomatist.* 1957

Paul Birdsall, *Versailles Twenty Years After.* 1941

Thomas A. Bailey, *Wilson and the Peacemakers.* 1947 (This volume combines two previously published works: *The Lost Peace* and *The Great Betrayal*)

III. IDEALISM AND REALISM IN AMERICAN FOREIGN POLICY

Hans J. Morgenthau, *In Defense of the National Interest.* 1951

George F. Kennan, *American Diplomacy, 1900–1950.* 1951 (or *The Realities of American Foreign Policy.* 1954)

Robert E. Osgood, *Ideals and Self-Interest in America's Foreign Relations.* 1953

Frank Tannenbaum, *The American Tradition in Foreign Policy.* 1955